PT
2635
.I65
Z657
1976b

6.00

Rainer Maria Rilke

A Centenary Essay

Timothy J. Casey

BARNES & NOBLE
BOOKS
10 East 53d St., New York 10022
(a division of Harper & Row Publishers, Inc.)

First published 1976 by
THE MACMILLAN PRESS LTD
London and Basingstoke

Published in the USA 1976 by
HARPER & ROW PUBLISHERS, INC.
BARNES & NOBLE IMPORT DIVISION

ISBN 0-06-491009-1

Printed in Great Britain

For Erika

Contents

Preface

Centenaries are traditionally the occasion for asking how still living and valid is the work of a poet. In the case of Rilke the signs have been unpropitious for some years past. The American Germanist, Heinrich Meyer, in his provocative *Was bleibt* seems to imply: not Rilke anyway.[1] Perhaps this is an unfairly abrupt summing up of his opinion for, while he does appear to accuse Rilke of 'Mache', it is more the productions of the Rilke industry to which he objects, irritated by the fact that the libraries of the world continue to extend the Rilke wing. In *The Truth of Poetry* Michael Hamburger comments on the Rilke scene: 'Four decades after Rilke's death the spate of publications continues as though nothing had happened; but more and more readers of poetry turn from Rilke's poetry with a feeling little short of disgust. The myth so beautifully sustained in his later poetry has been blasted by a barrage of biographical "indecencies"; the philosophy well and truly debunked by critical examinations.'[2] It goes without saying that Rilke is especially out of favour with the more politically and sociologically orientated school of criticism, as well as being, with a more summary kind of rough justice, the target of attack for all who would 'strike Germanistik dead, paint the blue flower red'. In the *Agitprop-Stück gegen das technokratische Hochschulmodell*, by Roman Ritter and Uwe Timm,[3] the play opens, after the inevitable 'Ordinarienbeschimpfung', with the first examination scene:

PROFESSOR *sitzend, einige Bücher in der Hand*: Welches Prüfungsthema haben Sie, Herr Candidat?

CANDIDAT *stehend*: Rilke, Herr Professor.

PROFESSOR *sucht eines seiner Bücher heraus, schlägt es auf, blättert, bis er eine Stelle gefunden hat*: Welche Folgen hat die Daseinssteigerung?

CANDIDAT: Wie Sie in Ihrem Buch 'Rainer Maria Rilke. Dasein und Dichtung' schreiben, ist sein Ergebnis eine Daseinssteigerung, so daß selbst das Schrecklichste einen 'großen positiven Überschuß' gewinnt und ein 'Dasein-Aussagendes, Sein- Wollendes' wird, 'ein Engel'.

PROFESSOR *verfolgt kopfnickend die Antwort, mit dem Finger die Zeilen im Buch nachfahrend.* . . .

All this is very unsettling, and one may mourn the fact that the very discipline of German Studies has so radically changed. You cannot, it would seem, serve Rilke *and* 'Kommunikationswissenschaft'. In any case, the centenary is an opportunity for re-examining approaches to Rilke's poetry, with all due caution in the light of so much scepticism.

The publishers and I wish to thank the following who have kindly given permission for the use of copyright material: Faber & Faber and Random House, Inc. for extracts from 'In Time of War' from *Collected Shorter Poems 1930–1944* by W. H. Auden; Insel Verlag, Frankfurt am Main, for quotations from Rainer Maria Rilke's work; Routledge & Kegan Paul Ltd for extracts from 'The Foreign Gate' from *The Collected Poems of Sidney Keynes*. The publishers have made every effort to trace the copyright-holders but if they have inadvertently overlooked any, they will be pleased to make the necessary arrangement at the first opportunity.

Timothy J. Casey

I Approaches to Rilke

Sola experientia facit poetam – so one might adapt Luther's dictum to Rilke exegesis, for Rilke's poetry seems to demand an understanding not unlike that demanded by Lutheran theology where, so the theologians would seem to agree, it is peculiarly necessary first to understand the Lutheran experience. Eudo Mason, the foremost Rilke scholar in the English speaking world, liked to quote Rilke's comment on the Belgian writer Rodenbach: 'man vergißt, daß es ein Gleichnis war, von einem Dichter erfunden für seine Seele, und man besteht auf dem Wortlaut.[4] Mason quoted with ulterior motive, for he was sceptical enough about Rilke's thought, caustic and iconoclastic in his attitude towards the general trend of the secondary literature, more especially where it concerned the favourite themes of Rilke hagiography, love and death, and saw Rilke's real greatness in an almost unparalleled sensitive gift for registering and communicating the most elusive sensibilities and states of mind. Mason's own approach may fairly be called biographical and he plainly indicated that to be interested in Rilke's work is to be interested in the personality of the poet and to take account of his life-style and his life-story. This is surely true. Even if it were a possible feat to feign a kind of objective disinterest in approaching a Rilke poem, it would be very forced and hardly worth the effort. If this is sometimes a limiting factor or seems to make special demands on the reader of Rilke's poetry, it is a small price to pay for its humanity. Of course the approach has its pitfalls. While centralising the art-experience is not to say, certainly not to decide in advance, that Rilke's art is 'Artistik' in the Benn sense of art experiencing itself as its own content and myth, now that the demythologising process has undermined other content, still there is a danger in concentrating so exclusively on artistic processes as the real frame of reference, whatever the Rilke poem may purport to be about. How fruitful an interpretation can be that deliberately eschews the assumption of a common denominator and a single overriding theme has been amply demonstrated by Anthony Stephens. Stephens takes many critics to task, but most of all Mason, doubtless because he was the most expert wielder of the appropriate Occam's razor, 'reducing all the apparent complexities and contradictions to the single theme of Rilke's own understanding of himself as an artist'. His own study, Stephens tells us, was written precisely 'in opposition to those critics who would make of Rilke's poetry nothing but one prolonged meditation on the difficulties of writing itself and who thus see every theme as a thinly disguised piece of aesthetic theory'. However, this is a loaded way of putting the opposition's case, and besides, when Stephens says that he took as his prime object not, obviously, Rilke's life, nor yet language in itself, neither 'Dichtungstheorie' nor 'das Sein des Sienden', but what he calls 'that admirable German invention "das lyrische Ich" ', one may feel that we are back with a concern not necessarily unlike that of Mason and others.[5]

An attitude apparently quite opposed to that of Mason is expressed by another of the most established and hardly less prolific Rilke critics, Else Buddeberg, when she says: 'Es war wohl selten ein Dichter, der so wie Rilke das rein Private völlig verschloß.'[6] Doubtless there is a real divergence of standpoint here and one that affects the ultimate views of the two critics, though again the contrast need not be so crass, depending on what one understands by the 'purely private', a phrase to be particularly cautious about in the case of Rilke, where life and work are integrated or at least entangled to a quite exceptional degree. One of Buddeberg's own main contributions to Rilke studies is, after all, a biography, albeit an 'innere Biographie'. It is true that Rilke speaks of the 'terrible polarité de la vie et du travail',[7] a theme as obsessively recurrent in Rilke's letters as in Kafka's diaries. But then there is the same bewildering combination in Rilke as in Kafka of on the one hand apparently ceaseless vacillation and on the other an unswerving dedication. Most critics have been struck by a curious absolutism not only of Rilke's poetry but of Rilke's being-a-poet. Edmond Jaloux records his impression on meeting Rilke:

> Quand j'eus commencé de causer avec Rilke, il me sembla que c'était la première fois que je parlais avec un poète. Je veux dire que les autres poètes que j'avais approchés, si grands qu'ils fussent, n'étaient cependant poètes que par l'esprit; hors de leur travail, ils vivaient dans le même monde que moi, avec les mêmes êtres; . . . Mais à mesure que Rainer Maria Rilke discourait, avec sa douceur et son admirable connaissance de notre langue qui a pu faire de lui un véritable poète français, il m'introduisait dans un univers qui était le sien et où je n'étais admis à pénétrer que par une sorte de miracle. Le féérique, le fantastique naissaient sous ses paroles : avec lui, j'échappais enfin à l'enfer du logique, au labyrinthe du possible.[8]

The French in particular seem to stress this. Of all the people he had ever known, says Valéry, Rilke was 'le plus mystérieux'. 'Si le mot *magique* a un sens, je dirai que toute sa personne, sa voix, son regard, ses manières, tout en lui donnait l'impression d'une présence magique.' And Gide says: 'On eût dit qu'il n'était jamais complètement présent dans son corps. On le sentait surtout ailleurs, dans une région mystérieuse plus réelle pour lui que ce que nous appelons la réalité. Et c'est dans cette région seulement qu'il se laissait vraiment rejoindre.'[9] It is hardly necessary to say that this is precisely what makes Rilke so questionable to some and that, predictably, German critics, more conscience-stricken and sensitive to the dangers of the so-called romantic tradition, are less happy to take leave of reality. Perhaps the most damaging polemic of this kind to date is the discussion of poetry and politics in Rilke in *Das verschluckte Schluchzen* by Egon Schwarz, who inveighs against just that Rilke, or just that understanding of Rilke, as one who inhabits a strange planet, not subject to the laws of our world, in the context of which his work is a beautifully useless Taj Mahal.[10] In a more restrained and qualified way the perils of the 'constant poet', generally and of Rilke, 'that almost mono-maniacally dedicated poet', in particular are discussed by Michael Hamburger in his essay on 'Absolute Poetry and Absolute Politics', which

ends with the sentence: 'Only very few poets opposed to the Roman-
tic-Symbolist aesthetic – usually on conscientious grounds – have
found it possible to be poets constantly; many more have lost
impetus not only because of economic or political pressures, but
because of a deep distrust of the autonomous imagination and its
atavistic affinities.' These, too, are damaging implications, only
that Hamburger's essay on absolutism is written in the non-
absolutist English spirit, finding the fault in ourselves if we seek
what we have no right to expect: 'To write great poetry is quite
enough for one man to achieve in this "disconnected world of
ours". That the truths of some poetry are partial and provisional
truths does not make them less valuable. It is up to the reader of
poetry not to approach it with expectations and demands which
it cannot, by its nature, fulfil.'[11]

This more pragmatic attitude suggests that one probably spends
too much time agonising over the admissibility of biographical and
other evidence extraneous to the poem itself, over the irrelevance
of intention or raw material when it comes to the finished product – questions that seem to be matters of principle, but that
often enough turn out to be a matter of common-sense decision
from one case to the next. Nobody can know in advance how productive the more author-orientated approach to a poem may be,
just as nobody can declare *a priori* the amount of biographical
material a poem can assimilate and communicate. One poem may
be richly laden in this respect without being, in its end effect,
blurred or lifeless, while a small amount of such material may be
dead weight in another poem. Rilke's poetry, at any rate, is very
allusive and on the whole not in the sense of learned allusions,
which in Rilke are in the main well-known cultural references and
for the rest so few in number one rapidly becomes familiar with
them, rather in a more self-referential sense of allusions to himself and to the history of certain ideas in his life, which so appear
in his poetry that the first impression we get of his work is the
striking recurrence of certain words and word clusters, which, like
'rein' or 'offen', are simple in themselves but obviously involve an
intensely personal and often enough idiosyncratic complexity.

Bollnow distinguishes between two methods of Rilke interpretation, the metaphysical and the existential.[12] He favours the latter, but is at pains to distinguish its universality from the all too narrowly biographical. Certainly the biographical can be both impertinent and banal. But it is noteworthy that Bollnow is speaking in the context of the love-motif in Rilke and to ignore the personal in this connection can be very misleading. The same is true of the death-motif, the concern of so much of the secondary literature and generally centred on Rilke's frequent assertions to the effect that life and death are one, particularly in the famous letter he wrote to his Polish translator explaining the Duino Elegies in terms of this 'unity of life and death'.[13] Whether the so-called 'Einheitslehre' is a useful approach to Rilke's poetry, even to the Elegies, is questionable. In theory one might imagine a poet so passionately convinced of this creed that the terrors of death are emotionally overcome, but in practice we find that the Elegies are in the first place elegiac 'Klagelieder', expressing with great sensibility and subtlety ideas of transitoriness and emotions of loneliness and loss. To be sure there are further dimensions in the Duino Elegies, but too often interpreters build on the basis of Rilke's theories, superimpose their own and move further and further away from the initial origin and impetus. An almost untroubled acceptance of death would seem to be a legend that has grown up around Rilke. In Ida Cermak's anthology *Ich klage nicht*, a documentation of experiences of illness, an attitude of piety on the part of Rilke is seen to be in contrast with more defiant attitudes of a rationalist like Freud or a revolutionary like Heine. But even here a false impression may be created. Cermak speaks of the sufferings of Rilke in the last stages of his leukemia:

> Rilkes langjähriger behandelnder Arzt, Dr. Haemmerli, sagte, Rilke sei nur noch ein armer 'Ausgeschundener' gewesen. Warum lehnte er hartnäckig jede Linderung durch Medikamente ab? Er war davon überzeugt . . . daß jeder seinen 'eigenen Tod' haben müsse. . . .

In the particular context it would seem relevant to note the account given by Dr. Haemmerli himself in a letter to Marie von Thurn und Taxis:

La pensée de mourir lui était tellement terrible qu'il l'écartait
au point de ne jamais même demander de quelle maladie il
souffrait et pas une seule fois il n'a parlé de la possibilité de
sa mort . . . son seul désir, était de ne voir personne qui eût pu
réveiller en lui la pensée de la gravité de sa situation qu'il se
cachait à lui-même volontairement. En effet, j'ai l'impression
qu'il attendait chaque matin ardemment l'assurance de ma part
qu'on pouvait le sauver. Avec son immense sensibilité le moindre
soupçon qui l'atteignait parfois si j'hésitais le faisait souffrir
davantage que son affreuse maladie et si on voulait le soulager
dans sa terrible situation c'était seulement en le tenant jusqu'à
la fin dans sa sereine idée d'une convalescence. On arrivait selon
son désir, à adoucir ses douleurs par des calmants sans lui faire
perdre sa connaissance.[14]

So far as Rilke's reception in the English-speaking world is concerned, it is interesting to note that Sidney Keyes regarded Rilke's
poetry as the culmination of the 'obsessional German death-wish'
and that Yeats was apparently estranged by what he took to be
Rilke's ideas on death, answering them with his own cold epitaph.[15] If this assumes an attitude towards death on the part of
Rilke which might fairly be called sentimental, it is a very mistaken
assumption. The tensions and complexities of the death-motif are
not the least part of the drama of Rilke's poetry, of the kind of
precarious balance so graphically expressed in this poem from the
Paris period:[16]

Tränen, Tränen, die aus mir brechen.
Mein Tod, Mohr, Träger
meines Herzens, halte mich schräger,
daß sie abfließen. Ich will sprechen.

Schwarzer, riesiger Herzhalter.
Wenn ich auch spräche,

glaubst du denn, daß das Schweigen bräche?

Wiege mich, Alter.

Certainly this is acceptance of a sort, but it is a very angular acceptance and a very oblique kind of lullaby, altogether typical of Rilke's involved manner. The drama continues to the end and to follow it is to feel in particular the shattering impact of that final poem, the last entry in Rilke's last diary[17]:

Komm du, du letzter, den ich anerkenne,
heilloser Schmerz im leiblichen Geweb:
wie ich im Geiste brannte, sieh, ich brenne
in dir; das Holz hat lange widerstrebt,
der Flamme, die du loderst, zuzustimmen,
nun aber nähr' ich dich und brenn in dir.
Mein hiesig Mildsein wird in deinem Grimmen
ein Grimm der Hölle nicht von hier.
Ganz rein, ganz planlos frei von Zukunft stieg
ich auf des Leidens wirren Scheiterhaufen,
so sicher nirgend Künftiges zu kaufen
um dieses Herz, darin der Vorrat schwieg.
Bin ich es noch, der da unkenntlich brennt?
Erinnerungen reiß ich nicht herein.
O Leben, Leben: Draußensein.
Und ich in Lohe. Niemand der mich kennt.

In the context of Rilke's poetry as a whole 'heilloser Schmerz' is a particularly terrible phrase, as Rilke tries to come to terms with a dimension of physical suffering that seems to introduce an altogether new hostility. As he says more explicitly in a further fragment: 'Das ist nicht so wie Krankheit war / einst in der Kindheit.' In his study of the general theme of suffering in Rilke, Falk rightly dramatises this final struggle, possibly indeed reading the poem in an over-hopeless sense.[18] In Rilke's struggle to remain true to his attitude of total affirmation there is, to be sure, a contrast to the more moralistic and rationalistic attitudes. But if there is any danger of misreading the poetry in any too easily affirmative spirit, recourse to biography by way of the last letters would certainly redress the balance, echoing as they do the 'Grimm der Hölle' and the threat of self-estrangement in this new and terrible form of anonymity. In December 1926 he writes to Frau Wunderly:

'Très Chère, jour et nuit, jour et nuit: . . . l'Enfer! on l'aura connu! Merci que de tout votre être (je le sens) vous m'accompagnez dans ces régions anonymes. Le plus grave, le plus long: c'est d' abdiquer: devenir "le malade". Le chien malade est encore chien, toujours. Nous à partir d'un certain degré de souffrances insensées, sommes-nous encore nous?'[19] To Lou Andreas-Salomé: 'Und jetzt, Lou, ich weiß nicht wie viel Höllen, Du weißt wie ich den Schmerz, den physischen, den wirklich großen in meine Ordnungen untergebracht habe, as sei denn als Ausnahme und schon wieder Rückweg ins Freie. Und nun. Er deckt mich zu. Er löst mich ab. Tag und Nacht! Woher den Muth nehmen?'[20] And to Rudolf Kassner: '. . . ich bin auf eine elende und unendlich schmerzhafte Weise erkrankt, eine wenig bekannte Zellenveränderung im Blut wird zum Ausgangspunkt für die grausamsten, im ganzen Körper versprengten Vorgänge. Und ich, der ich ihm nie recht ins Gesicht sehen mochte, lerne, mich mit dem inkommensurabeln anonymen Schmerz einrichten. Lerne es schwer, unter hundert Auflehnungen, und so trüb erstaunt.'[21]

Not that it can be said that Rilke literature neglects the biographical element. On the contrary, if there is one way of interpreting a poem that, broadly speaking, concentrates on the poem itself, as contrasted with another way in which the poet is in the foreground, then the body of Rilke criticism, arguably the most vast that has grown up around any modern poet, has been remarkable for the dearth of interpretations that might fairly be called work-immanent. This seems more a matter of instinct than of design. There is little consensus otherwise and the intention may be as iconoclastic in one case as it is hagiographical in another. But almost invariably, even when it is a case of interpreting a particular poem in isolation and regardless of whether the particular critic is enamoured with or disrespectful towards Rilke's wisdom and Rilke's world, the poem is placed in a peculiarly Rilkean context to a far greater extent than appears to be true of other poets. Indeed the reference to Rilke is usually further particularised and the poem is seen, not just by the specialist critic but by anyone tolerably well acquainted with German poetry, in the context of one or other stage of his development, of the period of the *Stunden-*

buch or of the 'Dinggedichte', of the Elegies themselves or of the post-elegiac final years. It is doubtful if the instinct to approach a poem in this way is as strong or as universal in the case of any other German poet one cares to mention. Even the so-called objectivity of those 'new poems' of his middle period, whose craftsmanship would most readily seem to invite a more author-effacing analysis, is invariably seen in the context of the particular biographical factors, of Worpswede and Paris, of the visual arts, of Cézanne and especially of Rodin. The instinct for this kind of reference is ironic in view of all that Rilke has to say, so often and so insistently, about the anonymity of art. He may speak of the ideal work of art as being 'without fingerprints', and he may have wished, as he averred, to 'say' a tree without any element of Rilke in it, but in any simple sense this is not true of any of his work, from *Mir zur Feier* to the end.[22] To be sure the so-called 'Dinggedichte' do have an imagistic discipline that contrasts both with the self-indulgence of his earlier work and the more directly self-expressive poetry of his later years. In retrospect Rilke himself gave his New Poems credit for more cold objectivity than they really possess, and criticism generally, perhaps too unquestioningly, follows Rilke seeing a turning-point in his career marked by the poem *Wendung*, which he sent to Lou Andreas-Salomé as an expression of a change he must accomplish and the theme of which is summed up in the lines: 'Werk des Gesichts ist getan, / tue nun Herz-Werk.'[23] But when Rilke in the New Poems with their so-called 'Sachlichkeit' turned to animals and things for the sake of their discretion and distance, it was to objects as media, focusing the concentration of the poet and giving him outer metaphorical equivalents for the 'inner event'. In a letter in 1907 he describes this creative contemplation:

Das Anschauen ist eine so wunderbare Sache von der wir noch so wenig wissen; wir sind mit ihm ganz nach außen gekehrt, aber gerade wenn wir es am meisten sind, scheinen in uns Dinge vor sich zu gehen, die auf das Unbeobachtetsein sehnsüchtig gewartet haben, und während sie sich, intakt und seltsam anonym, in uns vollzeihen, *ohne uns* – wächst in dem Gegenstand draußen ihre Bedeutung heran, ein überzeugender, starker – ihr einzig möglicher Name, indem wir das Geschehnis in unserem Innern selig und ehrerbietig erkennen. . . .

He speaks of things acting like a magnet, ordering the powers they attract, just as he says of his last landscape, Wallis in Switzerland, that it so wonderfully offered for an inner world 'manifold equivalents and correspondences'.[24] Or as he concludes in the more direct manner of his French poems: 'Car le verger et la route / c'est toujours nous.'[25] The term 'verger' reminds one of the poem in the second collection of the New Poems, *Der Apfelgarten*, which, with its ostensible subject and its localising subtitle, *Borgeby-Gård*, might lead one to expect the kind of objectivity associated with what we ordinarily understand by a nature-poem, but which in the event is very different in its self-referential concern for art and the fruits of art: [26]

Komm gleich nach dem Sonnenuntergange,
sieh das Abendgrün des Rasengrunds;
ist es nicht, als hätten wir es lange
angesammelt und erspart in uns,

um es jetzt aus Fühlen und Erinnern,
neuer Hoffnung, halbvergeßnem Freun,
noch vermischt mit Dunkel aus dem Innern,
in Gedanken vor uns hinzustreun

unter Bäume wie von Dürer, die
das Gewicht von hundert Arbeitstagen
in den überfüllten Früchten tragen,
dienend, voll Geduld, versuchend, wie

das, was alle Maße übersteigt,
noch zu heben ist und hinzugeben,
wenn man willig, durch ein langes Leben
nur das Eine will und wächst und schweigt.

It is a characteristic example of Rilke's craft of enjambment, though whether it is totally successful is another matter. The not only self-referential, but reverential tones of Rilke's poetry do not strike a sympathetic chord in all readers. For very politically orientated critics, like Egon Schwarz, the very mention of Dürer would be enough to evoke an allergic reaction to the reactionary attitudes they see in Rilke. But even readers less alert to political overtones might be disturbed by its half-lights and the rather precious abstractions of its inwardnesses, particularly as the whole weight of the poem rests on the abstraction of that one essential, 'das Eine', to which life must be dedicated and to which interpreters must devote so much explanatory exegesis. One feels that Rilke is less open to such criticism where he is more completely in his element, and his element is art rather than nature. In the more famous opening poem in the collection, *Archaischer Torso Apollos*, although its concern is substantially the same and although it, too, ends with a moral that is no less cryptic and discreet: 'Du mußt dein Leben ändern', the effect of its radiant art-image, the paradoxical totality of the torso, is altogether more graphic and hence its 'message' is more immediate.[27] This time the abstractions are left to the interpreters, who can only try to elaborate the message in whatever terms of concentration and collection, of intensity and integration, that seem least inadequate to express that total commitment and wholeness in every part that in Rilke are as much a matter of life-style as of attitudes to art.

But whether the image is taken out of art or out of nature, in Rilke it always reflects what is basically his constant concern, his own experience of poetic creativity. Doubtless there is a narcissistic element in this, but the experience is presented as something that points beyond itself. Rilke is firmly rooted in the German romantic tradition, in the tradition, for example, of Novalis, for whom 'Poesie', as the natural activity of the spirit, is a misleadingly special name for something that is rather the norm and eminently real. But whatever about the subsequent deductions, the first fact of Rilke's poetry is its own art and activity. It is in this sense that one feels the approach to Rilke must be a biographical one. It is not a question of identifying source-material, however interesting this may incidentally be. In any case, most particularly in the Duino Elegies, difficulties in detail are the least of the reader's worries. The real danger is that one should miss the wood for the trees, for of necessity the most thorough interpretations of the Elegies tend to become line by line explications that obscure their narrative and blunt their dramatic impact. The sort of material that is meant, therefore, in speaking of a biographical approach to the Elegies, is not that which might elucidate this or that detail, but that which highlights the drama of Rilke's life and work – and the high-points of both were the *Duino Elegies* and the *Sonnets to Orpheus*. The story of their composition, as reported in Rilke's letters, is not just source-material about their genesis, but concerns their substance, based as this is on the assumption that that experience of art which gave meaning to his life had a more than private reference. It is certainly a dramatic story, from the account of the first inspiration of 1912 to the final weeks of feverish composition ten years later. In her memoirs Princess Marie von Thurn und Taxis Hohenlohe, at whose castle on the Adriatic coast the Elegies were begun, sets the opening scene, as she recalls the day when Rilke seemed to hear a voice through the storm: 'Wer, wenn ich schriee, hörte mich denn aus der Engel / Ordnungen?'[28] In the event the ten elegies were to be composed over the next ten years and from the editorial point of view the story is a highly complex one, with consequential problems in interpretation that will perhaps never be fully resolved. But as it concerns the real impact and impetus of the Elegies, the story is also a simple one and ends with those euphoric letters he was able to write in 1922, to his publisher Anton Kippenberg, to Princess Marie and to Lou Andreas-Salomé. To the Princess he wrote on 11 February 1922:[29]

Endlich,
     Fürstin,
   endlich, der gesegnete, wie gesegnete Tag, da ich
Ihnen den Abschluß – soweit ich sehe – der
                    Elegien
             anzeigen kann:
                  Zehn!
Von der letzten, großen (: zu dem, in Duino einst, begonnenen Anfang: 'Daß ich dereinst, am Ausgang der grimmigen Ein-

sicht / Jubel und Ruhm aufsinge zustimmenden Engeln . . .')
von dieser letzten, die ja auch, damals schon, gemeint war, die
letzte zu sein, – von dieser – zittert mir noch die Hand!
Eben, Samstag, den elften, um sechs Uhr abends, ist sie
fertig! –
Alles in ein paar Tagen, es war ein namenloser Sturm, ein
Orkan im Geist (wie damals auf Duino), alles, was Faser in mir
ist und Geweb, hat gekracht, – an Essen war nie zu denken,
Gott weiß, wer mich genährt hat.
      Aber nun ists. Ist. Ist
      Amen.
Ich habe also dazu hin überstanden, durch alles hindurch. Durch
Alles. Und das wars ja, was not tat. Nur dies.
Eine, habe ich Kassner zugeeignet. Das Ganze ist *Ihrs*,
Fürstin, wie sollts nicht! Wird heißen:
      Die Duineser Elegien

On the same day he wrote in similar terms to Lou Andreas-
Salomé, this time telling also of the dramatic prelude, the 'Vor-
sturm' of the first sonnets to Orpheus, although for the moment
these are still overshadowed in his mind by the 'grace' and
'miracle' of the Elegies: [30]

... Jetzt weiß ich mich wieder. Es war doch wie eine Ver-
stümmelung meines Herzens, daß die Elegien nicht da –
waren.
Sie sind. Sie sind.
Ich bin hinausgegangen und habe das kleine Muzot, das
mirs beschützt, das mirs, endlich, gewährt hat, gestrei-
chelt wie ein großes altes Tier.

The rush of inspiration was not quite over. The 'radiant after
storm' was yet to come with the last written fifth Elegy (replacing
what is now published as *Gegenstrophen*) and, most marvellously
of all, with the completion of the totally unexpected cycle of fifty-
five *Sonnets to Orpheus*, the significance of which as the complement of the Elegies, Rilke only slowly realised and which he ever
afterwards referred to as a dictation he endured, an inspiration to

which he breathlessly submitted. At the end of the Hulewicz letter
he writes:[31] 'Elegien und Sonette unterstützen einander bestän-
dig –, und ich sehe eine unendliche Gnade darin, daß ich, mit dem
gleichen Atem, diese beiden Segel füllen durfte: das kleine rost-
farbene Segel der Sonette und der Elegien riesiges weißes Segel-
Tuch. Naturally enough it is particularly other poets who tend to
highlight the drama of Duino and Muzot. In Sidney Keyes' poem
for example, *The Foreign Gate*[32]

> Once a man cried and the great Orders heard him:
> Pacing upon a windy wall at night
> A pale unlearned poet out of Europe's
> Erratic heart cried and was filled with speech . . .

or in one of the sonnets in the sequence *In Time of War* by W. H.
Auden:[33]

> . . . When we regret that we were ever born:
> Let us remember all who seemed deserted.
> Tonight in China let me think of one,
>
> Who through ten years of silence worked and waited,
> Until in Muzot all his powers spoke,
> And everything was given once for all:
>
> And with the gratitude of the Completed
> He went out in the winter night to stroke
> That little tower like a great animal.

2 Rilke's *analogia artis*

Of the commentaries on the Duino Elegies pride of place must be given to that by Jacob Steiner, as the most essential work of reference and the one that for controversial points of detail provides the best summing up of the evidence and the arguments.[34] At the other end of the scale is the interpretation by Kreutz, possibly the shortest complete commentary.[35] Where Kreutz simplifies, Steiner complicates, and comparing the two, one feels that brevity helps, for Kreutz, far less detailed and in detail less dependable, communicates a greater sense of the drama of the poem, at once elegiac and jubilant. Some kind of law of diminishing returns seems to operate in the longer commentaries. Guardini's interpretation illustrates one method of coping with the problem, for his provocative commentary, so different to the usual neutral paraphrases, is an example of a very committed kind of approach to literature, carrying the reader along by the force of his own convictions.[36] Guardini tends to regard the work of art as a repository of truth that must be tested logically. He finds more to disagree than to agree with in the Elegies and, at the risk of being almost naggingly prosaic, harps on the theme of a 'depersonalised existence' that he finds in Rilke, seeing in Rilke's ideas the integrity of the human personality under attack. Thus he is unimpressed by the heroism-in-itself of the hero figure in the Sixth Elegy, that ideal of the unambiguous and self-contained, of a pure existence – 'Dauern / ficht ihn nicht an. Sein Aufgang ist Dasein' – untroubled by the realities of the human situation as it is otherwise expressed in the elegiac leitmotif: 'denn Bleiben ist nirgends'. The tenor of Guardini's argument suggests that in reality heroism has everything to do with 'Dauer' and that the meaning of the myths, whether of Siegfried or of Samson, is bound to their civilising purpose, freedom of man from monsters or of a people from op-

pression. Hence, Guardini persists in interrupting the flow of
Rilke's panegyric with awkward questions: sacrifice for the sake
of whom? heroism in respect of what? Guardini finds plenty of
humanity and heroism in Rilke, but it is, as it were, rather in the
more elegiac aspects of the Elegies, in the tormented questionings
centred on the person of the poet and his sensibilities towards
the realities of human life, rather than in the ideas and ideals em-
bodied in the figures of hero and lover. 'There is something futile
about this hero of Rilke's! His tragedy, like that of Don Juan, is
that of ultimate hollowness. To this extent he conforms closely
with Rilke's doctrine of "self-less" contemplation and objectless
love.'[37] Guardini would seem to imply that, perhaps because Rilke
projected an incapacity for personal relationships into the realm
of metaphysics, there is an essential emptiness at the centre of
Rilke's description of human existence which, lacking the reality
of I–Thou relationships, denies the core, the human person.
Such a suggestion of Rilke's as that we 'entzwein, indem wir da
sind', is for Guardini a 'monstrous' sentiment.[38] Any interpretation
of Rilke has to take account of this and similar misgivings. For
the moment one might suggest in passing that the sentiments of
the relevant Fourth Elegy are not that inhuman, not, that is to
say, if you relate its ideas and its ideal in the first place to the art-
experience. Arising out of discussion of the same material, H. F.
Peters, in one of the least doctrinaire of Rilke studies, comments:
'Clearly such an ideal does not represent the human norm. Rilke
is thinking here of the artist in the grip of his daimon, the artist
carried beyond himself by a creative upsurge. He is thinking of that
state of exaltation during which men speak with tongues; he is
thinking of what happened to him at Duino and what was to
happen again at Muzot. . . . But it is one thing to say that it was
a personal, even idiopathic, experience and another that it lacks
general significance. A considerable body of the folklore of all
peoples deals with "men possessed".'[39]

It is an obvious phenomenon of Rilke criticism generally that
many critics – Holthusen would be a notable example – quite apart
from dismissing Rilke's views on matters of practical politics, find
his ideas as such, ideas like those on the solitariness of love or on

the singularity of life and death, unacceptable and simply false, these critics in turn being taken to task by others for the irrelevancy of any such argument on the plane of ideas. In his introduction to the annotated English edition of the Elegies, E. L. Stahl is very sceptical of those many evaluations of Rilke's ideas abstracted from the purely poetic context.[40] Still, there is something to be said for what may seem less technically correct approaches, and there may be a greater danger of doing a disservice to the poetry in a too ready acceptance of ideas of openness and inwardness, totality and anonymity so long as they come in the form of poetic myth, than in the stubborn resistance to those ideas on the part of Guardini and others, whether in the name of a more personal God or of a more personal human being. Even with respect to the central orphic myth itself, that of 'song-existence' (Sonnets 2, III), one should not gloss over the difficulties:

Ein Gott vermags. Wie aber, sag mir, soll
ein Mann ihm folgen durch die schmale Leier?
Sein Sinn ist Zwiespalt. An der Kreuzung zweier
Herzwege steht kein Tempel für Apoll.

Gesang, wie du ihn lehrst, ist nicht Begehr,
nicht Werbung um ein endlich noch Erreichtes;
Gesang ist Dasein. Für den Gott ein Leichtes.
Wann aber sind wir? Und wann wendet er

an unser Sein die Erde und die Sterne?
Dies ists nicht, Jüngling, daß du liebst, wenn auch
die Stimme dann den Mund dir aufstößt, – lerne

vergessen, daß du aufsangst. Das verrinnt.
In Wahrheit singen, ist ein andrer Hauch.
Ein Hauch um nichts. Ein Wehn im Gott. Ein Wind.

'Gesang ist Dasein' is a formula that seems to run counter to the normal experience of art and life. To say that the mind of man is 'zwiespältig' may seem an unexceptionable commonplace. But to say: 'An der Kreuzung zweier / Herzwege steht kein Tempel für Apoll' could be regarded as one of those monstrous statements such as Guardini objects to, since it seems to take art out of the realm of all that we understand by the human person and interpersonal relationships. It is possible to accept too reverentially the truth of song as 'ein Hauch um nichts' in a way that relinquishes too lightly the more familiar life-art that Rilke seems so clearly and emphatically to reject – 'Dies i s t s nicht, Jüngling, daß du liebst. . . .' Perhaps one never can accept it, not merely not as the truth it claims to be, but not even as true of the Elegies and Sonnets themselves. In a sense the concept of art put forward here, the art of 'immediate' existence, beyond 'Begehr' and 'Werbung', beyond courtship of another and consciousness of self, is precisely not that art-medium of the Elegies born of man's opposition. Common to both Elegies and Sonnets and indeed to be found throughout Rilke's poetry is the theme of human alienation as expressed, for example, in the opening lines of another poem: 'Natur ist glücklich. Doch in uns begegnen / sich zuviel Kräfte, die sich wirr bestreiten . . .',[41] but it is rather the Elegies that face the human fate: '. . . warum dann / Menschliches müssen – und, Schicksal vermeidend, / sich sehnen nach Schicksal? . . .' (Ninth Elegy). Hence it may be easier to respond to the Elegies than to the sovereign claim of 'song as existence' in the Sonnets, or within the Sonnets themselves, to the more elegiac ones like 'Sei allem Abschied voran' or 'Wolle die Wandlung'. However, that is to oversystematise and over-conceptualise both Elegies and Sonnets. The greatest disservice one can do to the poetry is so to obscure it in speculative definitions of orphic 'Dasein' as to lose sight of the simpler drama whereby, in the Sonnets no less than in the Elegies, 'our existence' is expressed and affirmed: 'O Trotz Schicksal: die herrlichen Überflüsse / unseres Daseins, in Parken übergeschäumt . . .' (2, XXII).

Guardini's, at any rate, is by no means an unsympathetic study; it is only that the critic's sympathies are rather more strongly engaged on the side of the various neglected 'Thous'. Throughout he finds too much literature, too little life. The Fourth Elegy's description of the child's serene relationship with death seems to him sadly unlike the reality – as does the Tenth Elegy *passim*, for it is characteristic of Guardini that, where another Christian critic might be wary of the secularising Ninth Elegy but acquiesce more easily where Rilke becomes apparently other-worldly, it is the Tenth Elegy that Guardini is unable to accept, since the Christian cannot affirm death, which 'is but should not be'. All this is very logical and at times the logic is too much of a good thing, with too little regard for the fact that what Rilke has to say about 'Bezüge' in general and 'Liebe' in particular often refers, in the first place, to the artist's relationship to his material and his art, and that what he has to say about other things is largely by way of analogy to art and its processes. Thus it may be a true observation to say that in the Third Elegy Rilke confuses Sexus and Eros, but that hardly does justice to the poem, which is not so much logical as psychological and which in any case concerns the tangled undergrowth of adolescent confusions. It is possibly the simplest elegy in construction, the most single-minded in its intense self-centredness, exploring the jungle of feelings that seem to run rampant, not focused on mother or lover, but at the mercy of forces more atavistic and anonymous. The Elegy carries the conviction of its own kind of truth, which is not one that can be countered by accusations of narcissism or of distorting the I–Thou relationship. So far as accusations of that kind are concerned, Rilke often enough levelled them against himself. Besides, one would have had to have read Rilke very inattentively to be altogether surprised by the phallic tower and tree imagery of the posthumously published 'Seven Poems' – though they are certainly aesthetically startling in their so solemn and ceremonious imagery of erection and ejaculation.[42] Those 'Seven Poems', in which the beloved is apostrophised as 'Innen Geräumige', exploit the familiar imagery of space and inwardness in a grotesque fashion and are a strange variation on that theme of 'Innenraum' which is so very spiritualised in the secondary literature.

But viewing the Third Elegy less in isolation than in relation to the general structure of the cycle, what one notes in particular is the manner in which its material is finally referred back to the pattern of art-experience. The Elegy closes with the appeal for a counterbalance, for something to contain, as in a 'garden', the violence of the 'jungle':

... O leise, leise,
tu ein liebes vor ihm, ein verläßliches Tagwerk, – führ ihn
nah an den Garten heran, gieb ihm der Nächte
Übergewicht. ...
                    Verhalt ihn. ...

Like any long poem, if it is not to disintegrate into detail, the
Duino Elegies depend on response to an overall pattern. Here the
effect depends on hearing the echo of the same ideas and imagery
of human restraint and containment from the end of the Second
Elegy:

Erstaunte euch nicht auf attischen Stelen die Vorsicht
menschlicher Geste? war nicht Liebe und Abschied
so leicht auf die Schultern gelegt, als wär es aus anderm
Stoffe gemacht als bei uns? ...

Fänden auch wir ein reines, verhaltenes, schmales
Menschliches, einen unseren Streifen Fruchtlands
zwischen Strom und Gestein. ...

The Second Elegy is the one that most openly poses the problem
of human limitations, the inadequacies of transitory human life:

Denn wir, wo wir fühlen, verflüchtigen; ach wir
atmen uns aus und dahin; von Holzglut zu Holzglut
geben wir schwächern Geruch. Da sagt uns wohl einer:
ja, du gehst mir ins Blut, dieses Zimmer, der Frühling
füllt sich mit dir ... Was hilfts, er kann uns nicht halten,
wir schwinden in ihm und um ihn. Und jene, die schön sind,
o wer hält sie zurück? Unaufhörlich steht Anschein
auf in ihrem Gesicht und geht fort. Wie Tau von dem Frühgras
hebt sich das Unsre von uns, wie die Hitze von einem
heißen Gericht. ...

If the closing phrase of the Third Elegy, 'Verhalt ihn', echoes the
'reines, verhaltenes, schmales Menschliches' of the Second Elegy,
this in turn, which within that elegy echoes and answers 'er kann
uns nicht halten' and 'o wer hält sie zurück?, is an ideal and a

prescription for living suggested by way of analogy with the restraint of art as it contains and copes with the material of life. That the work of art indicates, or perhaps more properly, that the workings of art indicate a way of life is a conviction, conveyed by way of metaphor and the hidden links of imagery, basic to the Elegies.

It is undoubtedly a peculiarly self-centred centre of reference, and most Rilke critics speak in one way or another of the narcissistic or even solipsist elements in Rilke's poetry. Quite apart from the notorious theory of objectless love, which Rilke applied with such single-minded energy in every sphere of his life, from his domestic arrangements to his divine worship of a God who makes no demands as an object – so that even Rilke's angels are self-reflective, not mirrors of divinity in the sense of Dante's 'sono specchi', but, in the culminating and characteristically wilful Rilkean image of the Second Elegy: 'Spiegel: die die entströmte eigene Schönheit / wiederschöpfen zurück in das eigene Antlitz' – one must say that the Elegies are narcissistic at least in the sense that Rilke's own experience of art is the narrative thread running through them. In Rilke criticism, too, taking a very broad view of the vast secondary literature, there is a notable absence, let alone of the specifically sociological or political orientation, even of the broadly historical approach, or one might also say, as opposed to the lyrically egocentric, of the 'epic' approach. One may be aware of this lack, while at the same time feeling that in its general direction Rilke interpretation has quite naturally taken its cue from Rilke's own art and attitudes. His own political attitudes, for one thing, were for the most part determined by his instinctive recoil from any form of foreign interference, however benevolent, by his conviction that to each person is given the power to work out his own salvation in solitude and to cope with his fate, however terrible, so long as it is his own and not imposed from outside. Doubtless there is much wisdom in this, but it is true that Rilke is hardly in the tradition of the enlightenment and betrays little trust in any more rationalistic amelioration of humanity's ills. The often quoted phrase from a letter of August 1915: 'die Welt ist in die Hände der Menschen gefallen', is typical of an attitude that some may regard as inexcusably escapist.[43] It is an attitude evident in the Duino Elegies themselves from the beginning, with their scanty trust in man and his mastery of a world he thinks he has interpreted:

> . . . .
> Und so verhalt ich mich denn und verschlucke den Lockruf
> dunkelen Schluchzens. Ach, wen vermögen
> wir denn zu brauchen? Engel nicht, Menschen nicht,
> und die findigen Tiere merken es schon,
> daß wir nicht sehr verläßlich zu Haus sind
> in der gedeuteten Welt. . . .

One must admit that Egon Schwarz, in calling his treatise on Rilke's poetry: *Das verschluckte Schluchzen* (implying that Rilke swallowed the sob of protest at fascist injustice), has chosen a title that is felicitous as well as malicious.

Clearly those critics who, like Schwarz and Guardini, are most committed in their own approach, are the most critical of Rilke's ideas. Yet the very energy with which Guardini attacks Rilke's ideas has the effect of confronting the reader with the Duino Elegies as a vibrant work, just as it was probably the astringent criticism of Eudo Mason that did most to rehabilitate the poet after the reaction that followed the first Rilke-cult phase.[44] Mason had rather less patience than Guardini with Rilke's mission and wisdom and found even more distasteful any suggestion of art as a religious surrogate. He would seem to conclude that what really mattered most to Rilke was the life of the emotions as an end in itself, only – or so Mason would appear to imply – Rilke unfortunately did not always know this himself. It may be felt that, although some Rilke criticism is too credulous, Mason errs on the side of unbelief, that he is too casual in noting such details as Rilke's reference to rhyme as 'an infinitely affirmative yes', that Rilke's assumption of a world order in line with the laws and rhythms of his own creative experience was more than just an occasional tendency. It may well have been a pious illusion on Rilke's part, but Mason would seem to resist it too strenuously, so that he is led to regard the Elegies as an example of absolute solipsism and to cee something like a complete volte-face in the sonnets, rather than to accept both as a product of the same faith.

It is noteworthy, however, that the same violent separation of Elegies and Sonnets is to be found in the criticism of Dieter Bassermann, whose voluminous work on Rilke may be cited as a last example of the kind of engaged approach that seems to provide the best introduction to the Elegies.[45] Bassermann is very committed indeed and most other Rilke critics seem palely academic beside one so passionately involved. In his case, too, the defence of Rilke takes the form of attack, primarily on all those comforting Rilke interpretations which, whether they speak in terms of religion or of art or of both, end in some myth of redemption. Yet Bassermann's own Rilke – 'the other Rilke', to use the title of one of Bassermann's books – is a curiously mythical figure and Bassermann has to struggle to save Rilke, not only from his interpreters, but from himself. For the other Rilke of Bassermann is the poet of humanity's totally lonely heroism, the radical revolutionary whose poetry enshrines the tragic dignity of man 'in großartiger Voraussetzungslosigkeit' and 'ohne intellektuelle Hilfskonstruktionen'![46] There is probably no more wilful assertion than this in the whole of Rilke literature, yet Bassermann's projection of the fearless 'Diesseitigkeit' to which, he implies, Rilke won through, is a more vital approach to the Elegies than much of the scholarly commentary. However, to sustain his thesis, Bassermann has to contend with a great deal of Rilke's own work, not least with the Elegies themselves. Of the many ways of summarising the thought-content of the Elegies, one is to say that the whole cycle concerns 'Bewußtheit unserer Art', that it rings the elegiac changes on all that this involves and searches for a sense of purpose which it finds in that mission of 'inwardising' that only the 'oppositeness' of human consciousness makes possible. Ironically, however, Bassermann, Rilke's most passionate disciple, cannot tolerate the 'Auftrag' in the Elegies, tacitly admitting that this is indeed a 'Hilfskonstruktion' with which Rilke tried to evade the issue of his own elegiac insight, and hence Bassermann tends to champion the Sonnets, in which, in his view, Rilke stepped from the shadow of the angel into the clear light of Orpheus,

B

who is not a myth but, more honestly and simply, a symbol, whose death is not sacramental sacrifice, but symbolises the totally tragic destiny of man. One may sympathise with Bassermann's view, even feel that he goes to the heart of the matter, while being unable to agree with his underlying implication that the direction of the Elegies is suddenly deflected in a last-minute evasive action. The 'Auftrag' of the Elegies is no sudden construction – it is implicit from the very first Elegy: 'Das alles war Auftrag' – neither can it be extracted as an idea to be pronounced upon in isolation, for it derives its validity and force from the artistic experience in Rilke's life, which is also the material of his work, though in a more than private sense and with a more than personal purposefulness, extending the experience of rhyme and rhythm, pattern and order to a whole world-view of telos and logos and cosmos. Of course Rilke is a poet of the 'age of anxiety'. All the familiar terms of an acute crisis of faith, 'Angst' and 'Ausgesetztsein' and 'Geworfenheit', can be applied to the human situation as Rilke sets the scene in the opening lines of the Elegies, and Bassermann might wish that Rilke would rest content with the truly total isolation that seems the logical consequence (whatever about Nietzsche's own 'Hilfskonstruktion') of Nietzsche's 'der Mensch mit sich allein'. But Rilke had gone steadily along the path already indicated in the early diaries when he said: 'Wie andere ferne Welten zu Göttern reifen werden – weiß ich nicht. Aber für uns ist die Kunst der Weg. . . .'[47] The kind of godless conclusion devoutly wished for by Bassermann is just not in Rilke, certainly not admitted, and his world really is, or at any rate claims to be, 'full of relationships'. It is as if Bassermann were determined to have Rilke follow the logic, if it is logic, of Gottfried Benn, for whom the work of art really is an erratic artifact and unhistorical, vouchsafing the cold comfort of itself, but permitting no other comforting deductions from the aesthetic orders and satisfactions of the mind.

In this sense, however, Rilke is poles apart from Benn, for these are precisely the kind of deductions that Rilke tirelessly implies, so that what is most generally regarded as the main problem of the Elegies, whether their reference is primarily universal or individual, to man in general or the poet in particular and where the line is to be drawn between self-expression and 'Weltdeutung', is probably to be answered in terms of 'both – and'. The interpretative position is clearly stated in the article on the Elegies in *Kindlers Literatur Lexikon*: 'Hauptproblem der Interpretation bleibt die Frage, ob die Elegien als eine allgemein menschliche Lebens- und Daseinsdeutung (J. Steiner u.a.) oder vornehmlich als eine symbolische Gestaltung der individuellen Dichterproblematik Rilkes (E. C. Mason) zu verstehen seien.' The general trend of the Kindler article is to reject any reduction to the merely poetic and personal – not unnaturally, since Steiner wrote the entry. In the end the divergence in interpretation is probably not so crass, and one could still subscribe to most of Mason's insights, while on balance agreeing with Steiner. However, poetic readings are seldom a question of tidy logical divisions, rather a matter of how emphasis is distributed and one may feel that in his insistent reference to Rilke, Mason has placed the better emphasis, whereas Steiner, taking the larger view, too quickly leaves solid ground. Thus, in search of a point of orientation to explain the cyclic order of the Elegies, Steiner states categorically: 'Ihre Einheit gründet zunächst in der mythischen Symbolfigur des "Engels".' It is not, however, the angel that is the common denominator in all the Elegies, and it would seem better to take one's bearings from the omnipresent man, the lyrical 'Ich' whose concern is the same as that of the 'wir' for whom the Elegies claim to speak from the opening to the closing lines:

Wer, wenn ich schriee, hörte mich denn aus der Engel
Ordnungen? und gesetzt selbst, es nähme
einer mich plötzlich ans Herz: ich verginge vor seinem
stärkeren Dasein. Denn das Schöne ist nichts
als des Schrecklichen Anfang, den wir noch grade ertragen,
und wir bewundern es so, weil es gelassen verschmäht,
uns zu zerstören. Ein jeder Engel ist schrecklich.
Und so verhalt ich mich denn und verschlucke den Lockruf
dunkelen Schluchzens. Ach, wen vermögen

wir denn zu brauchen? Engel nicht, Menschen nicht,
und die findigen Tiere merken es schon,
daß wir nicht sehr verläßlich zu Haus sind
in der gedeuteten Welt. Es bleibt uns vielleicht
irgendein Baum an dem Abhang, daß wir ihn täglich
wiedersähen; es bleibt uns die Straße von gestern
und das verzogene Treusein einer Gewohnheit,
der es bei uns gefiel, und so blieb sie und ging nicht . . .

From the beginning the Elegies rivet the attention with their
extraordinary command of rhythm and melody, which allows
Rilke to take such liberties with language, the virtuosity of assonance and consonance that always seem so close to dissonance,
the confidence with which he can create a solemn poetic world so
self-assured it can contain the apparently awkward or angular
word, the apparently prosaic or legalistic turn of phrase. It is
basically a balance between conflict and harmony. The strident
'schriee' makes its dramatic impact at the same time that it is
entirely harmonised into the movement of the vowel music. The
human protagonist is brought up at once with a kind of antagon-
istic clash against the hierarchical 'Ordnungen' of the angel-world,
and throughout the Elegies, though they are creating their own
harmony, the main emphasis will be on the cry itself, on contrast
and conflict, whereas in the sonnets – for example in the closing
sonnet of the first part: 'hast ihr Geschrei übertönt mit Ordnung,
du Schöner', or in the twenty-sixth sonnet of the second part:
'Ordne die Schreier, / singender Gott!' – the greater emphasis
will be on the containment of that cry, on the order for which
the orphic legend itself is paradigmatic.

In the case of the Elegies it is not only a very dramatic but a
very self-assertive opening and the extent to which one feels it is
so probably colours one's readings of the Elegies as a whole.
Where, as in the case of Steiner, the interpretation is more
immediately metaphysical, this kind of emphasis is subdued and
indeed Steiner tends mostly to choose what appears to be the
less immediate interpretation. At one of the dramatic high-points,
the 'Hiersein ist herrlich' of the Seventh Elegy, he argues against

a one-sided emphasis on 'hier' and chooses rather to emphasise the second component of 'Hiersein'. In a more straightforward reading of the Elegies as a dramatic narrative, however, the emphasis, like the alliterative accent, seems rather obviously on 'hier', and to obscure this is to lose the force of that affirmation of 'Schicksal', in all its aspects of 'Gegenübersein', 'Gestaltung' and the rest, towards which the Elegies are directed in however roundabout a fashion. In the same way one feels that there is a greater sense of the personal tension of the poem in the shorter commentary of Kreutz, not to say in the still more personal approach of Bassermann, than in the exhaustive analysis of Steiner, when they discuss the closing lines of the same Elegy. However little attention one pays to the sequence in which the different elegies, in whole or in part, were written, it is difficult not to attribute a particular significance to these, the last lines to be written. Originally, the Seventh Elegy ended: 'Glaub nicht, daß ich werbe. / Engel, und würbe ich dich auch! Du kommst nicht: aus Rücksicht.' But when all the rest had been written, Rilke wrote the ending as it now stands:

. . . Glaub n i c h t, daß ich werbe.
Engel, und würb ich dich auch! Du kommst nicht. Denn
  mein
Anruf ist immer voll Hinweg; wider so starke
Strömung kannst du nicht schreiten. Wie ein gestreckter
Arm ist mein Rufen. Und seine zum Greifen
oben offene Hand bleibt vor dir
offen, wie Abwehr und Warnung,
Unfaßlicher, weitauf.

Here, as elsewhere, Steiner's analysis is extremely complete, but it also seems excessively abstract, and contrasts with the kind of dramatic peripeteia that Kreutz sees in his more summary view of the passage in the context of the confrontation of angel and man in the Elegies as a whole: 'Man muß die Verse der zweiten Elegie noch im Ohr haben: "Träte der Erzengel jetzt, der gefährliche, . . . eines Schrittes nur nieder und herwärts: hoch-

aufschlagend erschlüg uns das eigene Herz", dann ist zu spüren,
welch ungeheuerliche Umkehrung sich hier vollzogen hat.' If anything, Kreutz overstates the element of hubris, but it is significant
that Bassermann, whose approach is even more engaged and argu-
mentative, takes the same view, finding something almost offensive
in this sudden 'Überwertung des Menschen und Entwertung des
Engels'.[48] In fact the emphasis is not that sudden, and although
most interpretations tend to contrast the majesty and activity
of the angel-figure with the passivity and insignificance of man,
the Second Elegy itself, the one in which the angel is especially
celebrated and which most concerns the 'Grenzen der Menschheit',
opens on a characteristic note of self-assertion, conveyed by the
almost violent prefix, which poetically is the most forceful
element:

> Jeder Engel ist schrecklich. Und dennoch, weh mir,
> ansing ich euch. . . .

The complex of personal references is all the more revealing the
more interpretational complexities a Rilke poem presents, as in
the case of the Fourth Elegy, often regarded as the most difficult,
as well as, having been written at a nadir of his emotional life in
the autumn of 1915, the most anguished. The Elegy rings the
changes on the idea of discord – 'Wir sind nicht einig', 'Feind-
schaft / ist uns das Nächste' – on that existential 'Entzweiung'
that Guardini finds a monstrous view of life. There is, indeed,
something obsessional in Rilke's attribution of hostility to human
destiny and human relationships, often by way of contrast with
the world of early childhood, before consciousness has grown
and branched out into a 'Judasbaum der Auswahl', as in the un-
finished elegy that began with the lines: 'Laß dir, daß Kindheit
war, diese namenlose / Treue der himmlischen, nicht widerrufen
vom Schicksal. . . .'[49] With this grown-up world of choice only
the hero, the subject of the Sixth Elegy, can immediately cope,
where the poet himself comes to terms with destiny in a more
mediate way, in such total submission to the outsider-role of
observer that the apparent passivity compels the inspiration of
creative activity:

. . .
Dann kommt zusammen, was wir immerfort
entzwein, indem wir da sind. Dann entsteht
aus unsern Jahreszeiten erst der Umkreis
des ganzen Wandelns. Über uns hinüber
spielt dann der Engel. . . .

The reference of the Duino Elegies, as an elegiac on the theme
of 'Gegenübersein' and a search for a 'theodicy' that would justify
such a creation, is not restricted to that process of poetic creativity, for whose 'miraculous' transformations into the productive
and positive Rilke most usually uses the term 'Umschlag'. But it is
centred there, just as the problem of human consciousness is presented in artistic terms: 'Da wird für eines Augenblickes Zeich-
nung / ein Grund von Gegenteil bereitet. . . .' It is easy to mis-
place the emphasis of the Elegies, unless this orientation is borne
in mind, unless one recognises, for example, that if the role of
man in the Elegies seems very passive, this must be understood in
the context of Rilke's practice to speak of the artist, to whom the
God comes, the Angel or Orpheus, in terms of feminine receptivity.
     Wrested out of that context the ideas of the Elegies may seem
wayward enough, or even downright 'wrong', as witness the dis-
may of the Austrian philosopher, Rudolf Kassner, at the dedication to himself of the Eighth Elegy. In his summary of the
relationship between Kassner and Rilke, J. B. Leishman suggests
that to Kassner, whose own work implies a purposeful advance of
civilisation from the 'space-world of God the Father' to the 'time-
world of the Son', from identity to individuality, from magic to
freedom, from happiness to sacrifice, the Eighth Elegy, with its
longing for 'the Open', must have seemed a kind of atavism.[50]
Kassner speaks of Rilke's 'rancour' against the Son. This may be
to over-isolate the ideas of the Eighth Elegy, and the dedication
is not so perverse, if this Elegy is seen in the context of the whole
work and in its position between the affirmative and purposeful
Seventh and Ninth Elegies. Moreover, there is a constant over-all
pattern of attitudes in Rilke to which one must relate the particular

motifs of the Eighth Elegy, the evocation of what Rilke calls 'das Offene', 'das Reine, Unüberwachte' as opposed to 'Gestaltung', of pure 'space' as opposed to the closed 'world'. In spite of all the universalia and absolutes in Rilke's work, not to say in Rilke criticism, it is necessary to take account of the very personal factors that lend such obsessive force to his work and certainly do not take from its relative validity as poetry, even if it were true that they invalidate his work as something other than poetry. The Duino Elegies return again and again to peculiar ideas and ideals of life and love and the nature of Rilke's work leads much Rilke criticism not merely to centre on such themes, but to treat them as if they were not so much themes as theories, like the theory of 'anonymous' or 'open' or 'objectless' love, which in turn is bound up with all those other ideas of the anonymities of art and life. For criticism like this to introduce more biographical factors is unwelcome and perhaps felt to be not only indiscreet but irrelevant. Throughout his discussion of Rilke's 'open' love as opposed to what he calls the 'perspektivische Verengung der Welt auf die Geliebte hin'[51] Steiner tends to dismiss summarily not only any 'love-object', but any critic whose approach would be more relative than absolute and who would emphasise the personal element in these favourite themes of Rilke, even perhaps the element of special pleading. Granted the pitfalls in the approach, it does seem necessary to explore the course of such obsessively dominant themes in Rilke's poems and letters, in order to familiarise oneself with the experiences behind them. When one does examine the evidence, the pattern seems clear. Reduced to its simplest terms it involves an escape – if one does not use the term in too loaded a sense – from the betrayals and oppressions of the possessive in life to the liberating spaciousness of art. Although Rilke goes on to construct a whole mythology of living, based both on the experience itself of artistic creativity and on his understanding of art, it is in the first place a personal story that leads from the feeling of falsity, such as is expressed in the sentiment from the *Stundenbuch*: 'denn dort bin ich gelogen, wo ich gebogen bin', to the feeling of truth as expressed in a phrase from a letter to Lou Andreas-Salomé: 'wo ich schaffe, bin ich wahr.'[52]

3 *Denn dort bin ich gelogen, wo ich gebogen bin*

The poem *Östliches Taglied*, which, although the theme of love and figures of lover and beloved are so prominent in Rilke's poetry, might be regarded as one of the few love-poems, ends with the lines: [53]

Doch während wir uns aneinanderdrücken,
um nicht zu sehen, wie es ringsum naht,
kann es aus dir, kann es aus mir sich zücken:
denn unsre Seelen leben von Verrat.

In the Duino Elegies, the Fourth in particular emphasises the love-betrayal theme. A mysterious enmity springs up between the lovers, who betray the infinite promises they had aroused:

                                Feindschaft
ist uns das Nächste. Treten Liebende
nicht immerfort an Ränder, eins im andern,
die sich versprachen Weite, Jagd und Heimat.

In poem after poem Rilke brings together these themes of love and betrayal. In 'Die Liebende' for example: [54]

Ja, ich sehne mich nach dir. Ich gleite
mich verlierend selbst mir aus der Hand, . . .

. . . jene Zeiten: O wie war ich Eines,
nichts was rief und nichts was mich verriet. . . .

Or in a later poem from the Paris period: [55]

Ach die Pein der Liebesmöglichkeiten
hab ich Tag und Nächte hingespürt:

zu einander flüchten, sich entgleiten,
keines hat zur Freudigkeit geführt.

Reacting from this false or little love of possession and conse-
quent loss, Rilke develops his ideal of the unrequited, unpossessive,
solitary love. He expresses it, for instance, in the Requiem for
Paula Modersohn-Becker:[56]

> ... es ist zu schwer für uns,
> das wirre Leiden von der falschen Liebe,
> die, bauend auf Verjährung wie Gewohnheit,
> ein Recht sich nennt und wuchert aus dem Unrecht.
> Wo ist ein Mann, der Recht hat auf Besitz? ...

> Denn d a s ist Schuld, wenn irgendeines Schuld ist:
> die Freiheit eines Lieben nicht vermehren
> um alle Freiheit, die man in sich aufbringt.
> Wir haben, wo wir lieben, ja nur dies:
> einander lassen; denn daß wir uns halten,
> das fällt uns leicht und ist nicht erst zu lernen. ...
> Die Frauen leiden: lieben heißt allein sein. ...

Similar ideas are expressed, at great length and with stubborn
insistence, in many of the early letters, especially in the letters
to Kappus, the once so widely read 'Briefe an einen jungen Dichter'.[57] Beneath the smooth surface of these letters on the solitude
of love, there is an uncompromising rejection of any 'together-
ness' – 'das Aufgehen und das Hingeben und alle Art der Ge-
meinsamkeit . . .' – from which can only result: 'nichts als ein
wenig Ekel, Enttäuschung und Armut. . . .' 'Objectless love' on
the other hand is celebrated constantly in Rilke's poetry. Christ
refuses the love of Mary Magdelen 'um aus ihr die Liebende zu
formen, / die sich nicht mehr zum Geliebten neigt'.[58] As against
those saints whose love of God was too personal, who used Christ
'wie einen Beischläfer: als ein süßes Männlichkeitssurrogat, als
den zärtlichsten Amant, der zu haben war, endlich doch noch zu
haben war',[59] the ideal is rather the Portuguese nun, Marianna
Alcoforado, who said to her lover: 'Meine Liebe hängt nicht mehr

davon ab, wie du mich behandelst.' Thus, notes Rilke with satis-
faction, the man was discarded as a lover, finished, loved out as
a glove is worn out.[60] No theme recurs more often in his early
letters than this of the objectless love that is 'über jeden Geliebten
hinausgewachsen'. In Rilke's main prose work the theme and its
complement, the betrayals and dangers of love otherwise, are
determining factors of the narrative: 'Schlecht leben die Geliebten
und in Gefahr. . . . Um die Liebenden ist lauter Sicherheit. Niemand verdächtigt sie mehr, und sie selbst sind nicht imstande,
sich zu verraten.' Malte asks himself why Abelone did not direct
her love towards God, since she surely must have known that God
is no object or partner from whom a return of love need be
feared:

> Ich weiß, sie sehnte sich, ihrer Liebe alles Transitive zu
> nehmen, aber konnte ihr wahrhaftiges Herz sich darüber täu-
> schen, daß Gott nur eine Richtung der Liebe ist, kein Liebes-
> gegenstand? Wußte sie nicht, daß keine Gegenliebe von ihm
> zu fürchten war? . . . Oder wollte sie Christus vermeiden? . . .
> Seines starkbrechenden Herzens Linse nimmt noch einmal ihre
> schon parallelen Herzstrahlen zusamm. . . .'[61]

In one form or another this attitude reappears wherever Rilke
declares his view of life or of death, as in his many and, for all
the circumlocution, uncompromising letters of condolence. If
those who love one another must leave one another it is because
in the domain of love all that is worth while can be achieved
only by the solitary. Love is only apparently 'gemeinsam'; 'Gemein-
samkeit' breeds only 'Genuß', whereas real love is achieved only
by 'dem in seinem Gefühl Eingeschlossenen'.[62]

The biographical background to these themes is too obvious to
be ignored, whatever disagreement there may be about consequential problems of interpretation. The unpropitious details of
Rilke's childhood are well known: how in the earliest years he is
treated as a girl and how then, at the age of ten, he is sent, to
satisfy another family ambition, as a boarder to the military
academy. It remains a harsh story, not to be softened even in the
sentimental account of Elisabeth von Schmidt-Pauli, who amiably

attempts to turn it into an improving school story: 'Geist stand gegen Gewalt. Und der Geist siegte.'[63] Rilke could not bring himself to speak of those times for many years afterwards. When he did, it was in answer to a letter from one of his old teachers, General-Major von Sedlakowitz, who had written to ask the poet if he was the same pupil of thirty-five years before. After a long delay Rilke eventually replied in a letter remarkable for the force of pent-up feeling behind the elaborate, old-fashioned courtesy.[64] He describes how he had violently thrust aside the memory of those years, being unable to live with them, and how even now he can scarcely bear to think of them. He excuses his bitterness, declaring he was physically and spiritually abused and betrayed. It was inevitable that Rilke's attitude towards the communal in any form should have been influenced by those years. In his letters he returns again and again and with bitter insistency to the fervent wish that one must be left alone; and in fact he lived, as Jaloux says, 'comme s'il n'avait eu ni patrie, ni famille, ni postérité, ni religion même'.[65]

A late confessional poem on the 'Gewirr der Familie' is one of the more direct poetic reflections of his own childhood, thwarted by 'love', as the grown-ups disturb the solitary child, overpowering his personality and substituting themselves and their image of what he ought to be or think or do.[66] Rilke's 'open' love may mean much more, but it should not be unnecessarily obfuscated. Reaction against possessive love is very obvious, and it is not a particularly arcane matter, though experienced with extraordinary keenness by Rilke:

Liebe umkreist, die besitzende,
das immer heimlich verratene Kind
und verspricht es der Zukunft; nicht seiner.

Nachmittage, da es allein blieb, von einem Spiegel zum anderen
starrend; anfragend beim Rätsel des eigenen
Namens: Wer? Wer? – Aber die Andern
kehren nachhause und überwältigens.
Was ihm das Fenster, was ihm der Weg,
was ihm der dumpfe Geruch einer Lade

gestern vertraut hat: sie übertönens, vereitelns.
Wieder wird er ein Ihriges.

One could trace this theme throughout Rilke's life, in the story
of those relationships that we learn of through his letters. There
are many hundreds of those carefully composed letters. 'Absend-
bar oder nicht, gleichviel,' he remarks once of the letter form. He
cultivates a deliberate letter relationship – not least in the case
of his immediate family, in which the medium could combine
lasting concern with determined 'Distanz' – and welcomes the
freedom of an open correspendonce – '. . . nur damit die Distanz
da sei, die zum Schreiben nötig ist'.[67] In the letters of the earlier
years especially the keywords most constantly met with are such
as 'das Eigene', or 'die Einsamkeit'. Moving in its monotonous
insistency is the plea that he should be left alone to wrestle with
his own dangers and difficulties and that the disastrous distrac-
tions from without, masquerading as help and security, should be
kept from him. This remains Rilke's most heartfelt prayer and
could be extensively documented but, being a prayer, simple and
repetitious, it may be sufficiently attested by one quotation from
the closing years of his life.[68] In 1922 he writes to Countess Sizzo:

Ich meine, es müßte ein großes gewaltiges Gebet geben, des
einen Flehens, es möchte jeder nur sein Schweres auf
seinem Weg finden, ich will sagen, das, das zu den einmal
eingesehenen und leidenschaftlich bejahten Aufgaben seines
Lebens immerhin in einer gewissen Proportionalität stünde:
dieses dürfte dann groß, ja außerordentlich übermächtig, es
dürfte sogar tödlich sein. . . . Und ganz besonders, wenn man
an den Künstler denkt, dessen Aufgaben auf seinem eigen-
sten Gebiet ihn ohnehin völlig und unerreichlich übertreffen.
Ihm, vor allem anderen, wäre zu wünschen und zu ver-
gönnen, daß ihm (womöglich schon von Jugend an) nur
sein Schweres widerführe!

The determination on solitude is complemented by the conviction
that to seek refuge in relationships is guilty and turbid. 'Trüb'
and 'schuldig' are the adjectives most frequently applied to the

involvements and complications of human relationships. Again he
is repeating a lesson learned in childhood. He warns Kappus
against furnishing material for that drama of conflict ever played
between parents and children.[69] Even roles of rebellion are too
involved and instead of wasting his energy in trying to clarify
his position towards others, he should strive for the ideal of
solitude. When, in his own life, Rilke had sought companionship,
it was, he felt, an ominous sign and a weakness doomed to failure.
To Lou Andreas-Salomé he writes: 'Liebe Lou, es steht schlecht
mit mir, wenn ich auf Menschen warte, Menschen brauche, mich
nach Menschen umsehe: das treibt mich nur noch weiter ins
Trübere und bringt mich in Schuld. . . .'[70] He was nothing if not
sensitive to his own psychological problems, but when it was
suggested that he should consult Freud he no less rejects the inter-
ferences of psychotherapy. [71] If there is often nothing very unusual
in these attitudes, there is something obsessive in his relentlessly
repeated lesson that human relationships are at best troubled and
opaque. He learned that in his childhood, he writes, and how
often had he not found it reaffirmed when he saw people 'trüb und
aussichtslos verzwistet'. Although he regularly accuses himself
of failing to follow his own counsel, he just as regularly repeats
that his own particular conflict is the rivalry between art and
human intercourse. 'Alles Gerede ist Mißverständnis. Einsicht ist
nur innerhalb der Arbeit'.[72] He takes as his model the imperturb-
able Cézanne, whereas Rodin (with whom he had quarrelled) had,
he claims, at the end of his life failed his art through becoming
involved in a 'Schicksal' and therefore 'trüb'. 'Schicksal' is a
word of central importance in Rilke's work. Granted the danger of
abusing biography, it is well to remember how often the term is
used in the letters to refer to those 'foreign' complications, with
their threat of 'impurity' for which he has other names too, like
'das Verhängnis', 'le sort', 'le hasard'. Whatever the name, it is to
be avoided. 'J'appelle sort tous les événements extérieurs. . . qui
inévitablement, peuvent venir interrompre et anéantir une dis-
position d'esprit et une élévation solitaire par sa nature.'[73] References to these disturbances are to be found in every period of
Rilke's life, expression of determination to fly from false inter-

course to the pure celibacy of art. In terms of 'concentration' he exhorts himself constantly to imitate Rodin: 'Ich will mich sammeln aus allen Zerstreuungen und aus den zu schnellen Anwendungen will ich das Meine zurückholen.' To Lou Andreas-Salomé he sums up the lesson he has learned from his apprenticeship to Rodin: 'O was für ein Einsamer ist dieser Greis. . . . Sein tägliches Leben und die Menschen, die hineingehören, liegen da wie ein leeres Bette, durch das er nicht mehr strömt . . . Und ich glaube, Lou, so muß es sein . . . O Lou, in einem Gedicht, das mir gelingt, ist viel mehr Wirklichkeit als in jeder Beziehung oder Zuneigung, die ich fühle; wo ich schaffe, bin ich wahr. . . .'[74]

Yet Rodin himself is later found unfaithful to that solitude and Rilke speaks of the grotesque in Rodin's last years. Lou Andreas-Salomé observes of Rilke's relationship to Rodin that at the beginning Rilke surrendered himself 'wie man sich vermählt' and at the end was lacking in understanding and good-will.[75] But then Rilke's relationship to Rodin follows a pattern repeated over and over in his life. A closer look at the letters telling of his own experiences in and conclusions about human relationships reveals a disturbing parallel to those Rilkean 'theories' of life and love. Up to a point Rilke confesses his attitudes very openly. 'Was sind mir die nahen Menschen mehr als Besuch, der nicht gehen will,' he says in 1903 and years later he says of his acquaintances to Benvenuta: 'Solange mich ihr Menschliches nichts angeht, ists mir begreiflich und noch bis ins Grausamste hinein vertraut. Wo ich ihm aber je verpflichtet war, da hats mich gelähmt, da hab ichs nicht gekonnt.'[76] On this area of experience he writes with a bluntness unusual in his letter writing. 'Ein *Miteinander* zweier Menschen ist eine Unmöglichkeit . . . ,' he writes in one of those early letters on the topic of marriage.[77] While one does not feel altogether happy about the 'indecent' exposure of all this biographical material, it is no longer possible to analyse such Rilkean themes as 'Liebe ohne Gegenliebe' without some reference to his manner of life, or rather, more relevant to the poetry, his manner of speaking about that life. The particular details of those relationships, as confided especially in the letters to Marie von Thurn und Taxis and in which the most usual pattern is one of initial

euphoria and eventual disgust, are often obscure and probably of
no great relevance for the poetry. What is relevant is the moral
he so invariably and firmly draws. He writes to Princess Marie:
'Ah, liebste Freundin, es war eine Menge Wasser auf meine älteste
Mühle; wie sind die Dinge doch rein, die man in sich selber durch-
macht, und wie wird zwischen den Menschen das Gutgewollte,
das einmal Köstliche schlecht, schlecht, verdorben, ein Greuel.'[78]
No conviction is expressed more often in his letters than that all
that can come to pass between two people is 'trub'. 'Alles Unendliche ist innerhalb des Einzelnen.' The most innocent intercourse
is intemperate. Nausea is the invariable result of close contact,
even to be looked at is to be 'paralysed', and the only ideal is
utter reserve. In its very nature as need for another Eros is 'not
beautiful', and he frequently returns to the theme, all the more
striking in view of his general confession of faith in nature, that in
the erotic sphere nature betrays into surrender and communion:
'Aber denke doch nur, kann das etwas Schönes sein, sich fort-
zugeben . . . nein, sie kann es nicht . . . keiner von den beiden
hat mehr etwas Unzerschlagenes, Reines und Unverdorbenes um
sich.'[79] To Benvenuta in particular he unburdened his feelings of
'abuse':

> Ach, wenn ich Dir davon spreche, Benvenuta, von diesem
> Schlechtwerden, bis weit in die Seele hinein, und den ganzen
> Körper entlang. Diesem Verbogenwerden, wie ein Ding, das man
> verwendet zu nicht ihm entsprechenden Gebräuchen – Ben-
> venuta, Du würdest es nicht glauben, welche Häßlichkeit mir
> beim Anblick menschlicher Verhältnisse kann durch die Seele
> gehen.[80]

The book in which 'Benvenuta' herself, Magda von Hattingberg,
gives an account of their relationship, has been much attacked
for misrepresenting Rilke. When she records her reaction to the
Elegies, her feeling of their 'complete hostility to life', it is easy –
and true – to say that on the contrary Rilke spent his life affirming
life. Yet it is hardly such an insensitive reaction to the Elegies.
    There are many other examples, but to follow their course
would be to go over the same ground. Probably the letters to

'Merline', Baladine Klossowska, are those one first thinks of as Rilke's 'love-letters', but they are also the letters in which he most emphasises what he calls his 'Verhängnis'. With respect to this relationship, too, the reproaches in the end centre on the loss of that innocent state of 'Arglosigkeit' – one of the recurring key-terms in the word-cluster of Rilkean openness. The most frequent theme of the letters to Merline is the 'terrible polarité de la vie et du travail', that 'combat atroce', the almost unnatural sacrifices demanded by a life of art: 'Qu'elle est tenace, qu'elle est insensée.' It is a theme more unsparingly expressed by Rilke himself in these letters than by any of his critics: 'La vie de tout homme qui est arrivé à un certain point de son engagement avec l'art, subit des défigurations qui, d'un certain côté l'approchent du maniaque.' The fear of 'la violence' is as strong as ever, the determination to remain 'au-dessus des dangers banaux'.[81] It may have been bitter for Merline to find him rejecting so bluntly, even with irritation, her statement that 'life gave him everything', since he had said it often enough himself. But he wishes to underline that 'real' life invariably betrays. He can only hope that they will succeed in avoiding any 'Schicksal' whatsoever.

Das Leben ist nicht für mich diejenige Macht, die, wie Du schreibst, 'm'a tout donné' – wo andere die Gabe gewahrten, da empfand ich nur das Gewicht . . . Nach allem, was ich je erfahren habe . . . kann ich nur wünschen, daß das Schicksal nichts mit uns vorhabe (wir sind kein Stoff für es), sondern daß wir, außerhalb seiner immer wieder, was ja seit je das Wesen unserer Entzückung war, uns eine fast göttliche Entrückung zu erweisen vermöchten, irgendwo auf Inseln im Raum, auf denen es nicht die gewöhnliche Schwerkraft gibt.

His partner must even bear the reproach of having spoken of his Elegies as 'his work', though again she had only used a term which she had every reason to believe was sacred to him. But he wishes to emphasise that the 'work' of the artist is primarily a matter of receptivity in solitude '. . . aber die Entscheidungen fallen nun im Alleinsein'.[82]

If all of this has bearing on poetic motifs, the correspondence with Erika Mitterer, finally, is itself part of the poetic work. 'Ich bin jener, den man nicht erreicht / und im Recht nur, wo ich mich erwehre. / Dicht an Deinem Herzen wär ich Schwere, / aber aus der Ferne mach ich leicht.' Here, no less than elsewhere, 'Angst der Verborgenheit' is an obsessively recurrent theme, though now it appears more often by way of the counterpart theme of freedom – 'frei zu sein von Maßen und von Jahren...'. Without overstating the structural unity of the correspondence, it could be said to develop the concept of the two spheres, 'Wirklichkeit' and 'das ganz Imaginäre', introduced in the first letter:[83]

Daß Du bist genügt. Ob ich nun wäre,
laß es zwischen uns in Schwebe sein.
Wirklichkeit ist wahr in ihrer Sphäre;
schließlich schließt das ganz Imaginäre
alle Stufen der Verwandlung ein....

Soll mich nun dafür der Zweifel ätzen,
ob Du wirklich bist, die zu mir spricht?
Ach, wie wir das Unbekannte schätzen:
nur zu rasch, aus Gleich- und Gegensätzen,
bildet sich ein liebes Angesicht!

The letter poems to Erika Mitterer are a particularly obvious example of the transformation from 'Wirklichkeit' into those various poetic motifs of the open and pure or the closed and perverted. The transformation is, indeed, very complete and some of these brief poems would be difficult to decipher without reference to the development of their ideas in a lifelong personal history.[84]

Vertraust Du so? Nicht meine Demut nur,
mein Wesen zittert vor so viel Vertrauen.
Mein Grund ist zu geheim, um drauf zu bauen;
ich bin Gefahr, sonst wär ich nicht Natur.

Doch weißt Du's nicht? Sooft es selig war,
rief Dir Dein Blut nicht immer feierlicher:
Gewagtes Kind, nun bist Du nirgends sicher
als in Gefahr.

The kernel of the poem is the concept of 'Gefahr' and that 'Wagnis', which is its acceptance and accomplishment. Hence it introduces a motif crucial to some of the major poems like *Ausgesetzt auf den Bergen des Herzens* . . . and *Wie die Natur die Wesen überläßt* . . . , so often discussed in Rilke literature.[85] The latter poem is central to the famous Rilke analysis by Heidegger, with its questionable etymologies and virtuoso variations of 'wagen', 'wiegen', 'wägen', and 'wegen'. In discussing matters like Rilke's reaction to the modern world, Heidegger interposes the further difficulty of his own language:[86] 'Die unbedingte Einrichtung des bedingungslosen Sichdurchsetzens der vorsätzlichen Herstellung der Welt in den Zustand des menschlichen Befehls ist ein Vorgang, der aus dem verborgenen Wesen der Technik hervorkommt.' Often it may be a good general principle to trust to an over-all reading of poems like these, without presupposing great obscurity. The first of the poems, written in 1914 is more single-minded in its description of the exposed position of man's knowingness against the background of a world that appears otherwise 'heil', 'gesichert', 'geborgen'.

Ausgesetzt auf den Bergen des Herzens. Siehe, wie klein dort,
siehe: die letzte Ortschaft der Worte, und höher,
aber wie klein auch, noch ein letztes
Gehöft von Gefühl. Erkennst du's?
Ausgesetzt auf den Bergen des Herzens. Steingrund
unter den Händen. Hier blüht wohl
einiges auf; aus stummem Absturz
blüht ein unwissendes Kraut singend hervor.
Aber der Wissende? Ach, der zu wissen begann
und schweigt nun, ausgesetzt auf den Bergen des Herzens.
Da geht wohl, heilen Bewußtseins,
manches umher, manches gesicherte Bergtier,
wechselt und weilt. Und der große geborgene Vogel
kreist um der Gipfel reine Verweigerung. – Aber
ungeborgen, hier auf den Bergen des Herzens. . . .

The second poem was written in 1924 and is characterised by the more affirmative celebration of that human life that is 'um einen

Hauch wagender', by that later emphasis in Rilke on the 'will to exposure', which is the very breath of man's life and art:

Wie die Natur die Wesen überläßt
dem Wagnis ihrer dumpfen Lust und keins
besonders schützt in Scholle und Geäst:
so sind auch wir dem Urgrund unseres Seins
nicht weiter lieb; e r   w a g t   u n s. Nur daß wir,
mehr noch als Pflanze oder Tier,
m i t diesem Wagnis gehn; es wollen; manchmal auch
wagender sind (und nicht aus Eigennutz)
als selbst das Leben ist – , um einen Hauch
wagender.... Dies schafft uns, außerhalb von Schutz,
ein Sichersein, dort wo die Schwerkraft wirkt
der reinen Kräfte; was uns schließlich birgt
ist unser Schutzlossein und daß wir's so
in's Offne wandten, da wir's drohen sahen,
um es, im weitsten Umkreis, irgendwo,
wo das Gesetz uns anrührt, zu bejahen.

One can make this poem the starting-point for wide-ranging discussion of Rilke's Weltanschauung but in the personal context of Rilke's development one recognises in the first place how this grandiose celebration of 'Schutzlossein' develops out of that theme of a falsely distorting 'protectiveness' against which Rilke reacts with such passion. Rilke literature tends to arrive very quickly at remote regions of Being, if not indeed to start from there. One feels, however, that in the case of a poem like this its 'metaphysical' theme of the 'will to be' derives its force from that intensely personal sense in which Rilke so often celebrates a Nature that cares for her creatures in that, above all, she 'lets them *be*'.

The danger apostrophised in the poem to Erika Mitterer is conceived of as necessary and natural, the defencelessness of life itself, at once 'geborgen' and 'ausgesetzt', exposed to its own mysteries, above all the mystery of death. It is not 'danger' of the kind referred to in the passage quoted from *Malte*: 'Schlecht

leben die Geliebten und in Gefahr. . . .'[87] This is one of the many
– and all interrelated – distinctions between the 'great' and the
'little', common to so many Rilke motifs. The belittling danger
is not 'necessary', but rather the 'ungefähre Gefahr' of those
betrayals that are such a persistent motif in Rilke's poetry. Apart
from the term 'Verrat' itself the history of various synonymous
terms, particularly perhaps the term 'Lüge', suggests how the
theme develops. A veritable leitmotif is expressed in the sentence
from the *Stundenbuch*:

> Denn dort bin ich gelogen, wo ich gebogen bin.

In the early poetry it is a more one-sided theme of hostility or
the betrayal of promise:[88]

> Sieh dir die Liebenden an,
> wenn erst das Bekennen begann,
> wie bald sie lügen.

Later the 'lying' form of danger comes to be contrasted with the
'pure' danger of life itself that shelters those who totally entrust
themselves to it:[89]

> Denn wer begriffe nicht, daß die Hände der Hütung
> lügen, die schützenden – , selber gefährdet. . . .
>   . . . Dennoch!
> Was du da nennst, das i s t die Gefahr, die ganze
> reine Gefährdung der Welt – , und so schlägt sie in Schutz um,
> wie du sie rührend erfühlst. Das innige Kindsein
> steht wie die Mitte in ihr, sie a u s -fürchtend, furchtlos.

In the poems of the last years, for example in: 'Brau uns den
Zauber, in dem die Grenzen sich lösen . . .'[90] the theme is given
a wider significance in the sense that man is felt to be threatened,
not only by alien protection, but by his own consciousness, by the
consciousness of time itself, tempting him to make invalid
distinctions that prevent him from accepting the totality of life:

> Löse mit einigen Tropfen das Engende jener
> Grenze der Zeiten, die uns belügt. . . .

For Rilke, most of all in the latest poems, art is such a magic
alembic through which transitoriness is experienced as transformation, an experience of 'Vollzähligkeit', not of loss and betrayal:[91]

> Wie sich Geschehenes im Raum verfügt:
> Eines ward Wiese, eines ward Baum, eins ging
> den Himmel bilden helfen. . . . Schmetterling
> und Blume sind vorhanden, keines lügt;
> Verwandlung ist nicht Lüge. . . .

The German Romantic tradition has always stressed a paradoxical
understanding of art as at once so 'unheimlich' and so 'heimlich'
and precisely where Rilke's theme is the 'magic' of art, as in the
poem *Magie*, he stresses its 'reality':[92]

> Aus unbeschreiblicher Verwandlung stammen
> solche Gebilde – : Fühl! und glaub!
> Wir leidens oft: zu Asche werden Flammen;
> doch in der Kunst: zur Flamme wird der Staub.
>
> Hier ist Magie. In das Bereich des Zaubers
> scheint das gemeine Wort hinaufgestuft . . .
> und ist doch wirklich wie der Ruf des Taubers,
> der nach der unsichtbaren Taube ruft.

The image of the dove reappears in the last poem to Erika
Mitterer, which returns once more to the idea of danger and its
enrichment, symbolised in the flight of the dove as in the flight
of the ball, as opposed to the impoverishment of apparent protectiveness.[93]

> Taube, die draußen blieb   außer dem Taubenschlag,
> wieder in Kreis und Haus,   einig der Nacht, dem Tag,
> weiß sie die Heimlichkeit,   wenn sich der Einbezug
> fremdester Schrecken schmiegt in den gefühlten Flug.
>
> Unter den Tauben, die   allergeschonteste,
> niemals gefährdetste,   kennt nicht die Zärtlichkeit;
> wiedererholtes Herz   ist das bewohnteste:
> freier durch Widerruf   freut sich die Fähigkeit.

Über dem Nirgendssein   spannt sich das Überall!
Ach der geworfene,   ach der gewagte Ball,
füllt er die Hände nicht   anders mit Wiederkehr:
rein um sein Heimgewicht   ist er mehr.

In the Duino Elegies the same pattern of contrast between an
open increase and an enclosed belittlement is basic to the love-
motif. In the First Elegy:

... Ist es nicht Zeit, daß wir liebend
uns vom Geliebten befrein und es bebend bestehn:
wie der Pfeil die Sehne besteht, um gesammelt im Absprung
m e h r zu sein als er selbst, denn Bleiben ist nirgends. . . .

The Second Elegy returns to the theme of the promise of 'Dauer'
and its betrayal:

... Und doch, wenn ihr der ersten
Blicke Schrecken besteht und die Sehnsucht am Fenster,
und den ersten gemeinsamen Gang, e i n Mal durch den Garten:
Liebende, s e i d ihrs dann noch? Wenn ihr einer dem andern
euch an den Mund hebt und ansetzt – : Getränk an Getränk:
o wie entgeht dann der Trinkende seltsam der Handlung.

In so far as one can speak of 'answers' in the Elegies, they are
answers by way of re-viewing the questions themselves. If man
can neither 'remain' nor 'possess', then the Elegies and Sonnets, just as they equate 'Bleiben' with 'Erstarrung' – (Sonnets 2, XII): 'Was sich ins Bleiben verschließt, schon i s t s das
Erstarrte . . .' – so too they reject the 'possessiveness' of possession. If so much of the ideal of an open, objectless love can
thus, and so obviously, be referred back to almost obsessive fears
of 'Besitz' and 'Lüge' of being 'verraten' and 'verbogen', it may
appear that the poetry is deriving its insight from experiences that
are themselves distorted and unhappy. But the myth of life as
developed in the Duino Elegies is something different again from
those impulses, although it is true that its poetic force does derive
from there, just as it appeals to the personal experience of art
to suggest how the tensions and conflicts of life might be resolved:

Erstaunte euch nicht auf attischen Stelen die Vorsicht
menschlicher Geste? war nicht Liebe und Abschied
so leicht auf die Schultern gelegt, als wär es aus anderm
Stoffe gemacht als bei uns? Gedenkt euch der Hände,
wie sie drucklos beruhen, obwohl in den Torsen die Kraft steht.

If the Elegies in general are concerned with the limitations of
life as the human consciousness experiences it, with feelings of
transitoriness and oppositeness, this Second Elegy in particular
is constructed around the contrast between 'angelic' and human
existence, which is to some extent a contrast between spatial
and temporal images, but is also a contrast between images of
evaporation and the cycle of angelic 'outstreaming' that returns
to itself:

Frühe Geglückte, ihr Verwöhnten der Schöpfung,
Höhenzüge, morgenrötliche Grate
aller Erschaffung, – Pollen der blühenden Gottheit,
Gelenke des Lichtes, Gänge, Treppen, Throne,
Räume aus Wesen, Schilde aus Wonne, Tumulte
stürmisch entzückten Gefühls und plötzlich, einzeln,
S p i e g e l: die die enströmte eigene Schönheit
wiederschöpfen zurück in das eigene Antlitz.

Denn wir, wo wir fühlen, verflüchtigen; ach wir
atmen uns aus und dahin; . . .

The mythical figure of the Angel and the mythical motif of the
'Auftrag' are probably the most memorable elements of the
Elegies, but to concentrate on them tends to deflect from the most
constructive aspect of the cycle, the transformation of those themes
of evaporation and oppositeness into themes of relationship and
permanence. Grounded in the poetic experience itself, the sense
of permanence and achievement is most dominant in the post-
elegiac poems, beginning with the Sonnets to Orpheus. To some
extent the contrast between Elegies and Sonnets is a contrast between images of space and images of time, for as opposed to the
elegiac emphasis on exclusion and loss, the Sonnets are from

the beginning dominated by a sense of spaciousness and integration:

Da stieg ein Baum. O reine Übersteigung!
O Orpheus singt! O hoher Baum im Ohr!

But again it is not so much a question of contrasting space and
time images as of different modes of expressing the same time-
conditioned experience. It is often said that the Sonnets complement the Elegies and this is particularly true of the second
sequence of Sonnets, the series written after the Elegies had been
completed. That sequence begins with the elegiac motif of breathing, but now in terms of rhythm and relationship in a world itself
'voller Bezüge':

Atmen, du unsichtbares Gedicht!
immerfort um das eigne
Sein rein eingetauschter Weltraum. Gegengewicht,
in dem ich mich rhythmisch ereigne.

Einzige Welle, deren
allmähliches Meer ich bin;
sparsamste du von allen möglichen Meeren, –
Raumgewinn.

Wieviele von diesen Stellen der Räume waren schon
innen in mir. Manche Winde
sind wie mein Sohn.

Erkennst du mich, Luft, du, voll noch einst meiniger Orte?
Du, einmal glatte Rinde,
Rundung und Blatt meiner Worte.

While the Elegies and Sonnets overlap with, as much as they
complement, each other, it is true that in the Elegies the dark
theme of 'Gegenübersein' dominates, in the Sonnets the radiant
theme of 'Bezug'. The motif of breathing in the Elegies mainly
suggests transitoriness (Second Elegy): 'Denn wir, wo wir fühlen,
verflüchtigen; ach wir / atmen uns aus und dahin . . .' – and the
'pure' breath of life is an ideal of integration outside the 'world'
of ordinary experience (Eighth Elegy): 'Immer ist es Welt /
und

niemals Nirgends ohne Nicht: das Reine / Unüberwachte, das man atmet und / unendlich w e i ß und nicht begehrt.' But, in one of the many variations of 'Umschlag', the motif of breathing, which had suggested the transitory and finite, also suggests the 'infinity' of transformation and relationship, and what had appeared a loss in terms of time is, as it were, an increase of space, a theme already tentatively proposed in the very first Elegy:

> . . . Wirf aus den Armen die Leere
> zu den Räumen hinzu, die wir atmen; vielleicht daß die Vögel
> die erweiterte Luft fühlen mit innigerem Flug.

It is, however, in the Sonnets and particularly in the later sequence, that this theme of 'Raumgewinn' is developed, as in the opening sonnet, quoted above, or again and finally, in the closing sonnet, where Rilke urges once more an attitude of total openness towards the unending transformations of life, an attitude taken over from the experience of art and its paradoxical promise of personal fulfilment in the midst of anonymity:

> Stiller Freund der vielen Fernen, fühle,
> wie dein Atem noch den Raum vermehrt.
> Im Gebälk der finstern Glockenstühle
> laß dich läuten. Das, was an dir zehrt,
>
> wird ein Starkes über dieser Nahrung.
> Geh in der Verwandlung aus und ein.
> Was ist deine leidendste Erfahrung?
> Ist dir Trinken bitter, werde Wein.
>
> Sei in dieser Nacht aus Übermaß
> Zauberkraft am Kreuzweg deiner Sinne,
> ihrer seltsamen Begegnung Sinn.
>
> Und wenn dich das Irdische vergaß,
> zu der stillen Erde sag: ich rinne.
> Zu dem raschen Wasser sprich: ich bin.

If the sense of integration dominates in the Sonnets, this is related to the aural figure of Orpheus, whose medium is music, as

opposed to the vision of the Angel, and to a large extent the
contrast between Elegies and Sonnets depends on the suggestion
that the act of seeing accentuates the sense of 'distance', where
the world of Orpheus passes into and becomes part of those who
are conscious of its music – as in Rilke's poetry generally music
is the most mysteriously integrating and synaesthetic art. For
example in *Musik*: [94]

Irgendwo s t e h t Musik, wie irgendwo
dies Licht in Ohren fällt als fernes Klingen . . .
für unsre Sinne einzig scheint das so
getrennt. . . .

Or in *An die Musik*: [95]

Musik: Atem der Statuen. Vielleicht:
Stille der Bilder. Du Sprache wo Sprachen
enden. Du Zeit,
die senkrecht steht auf der Richtung
vergehender Herzen.
Gefühle zu wem? O du der Gefühle
Wandlung in was? – in hörbare Landschaft.

Even Orpheus is, as it were, too definitive and almost divisive
a figure (Sonnets 1, V):

. . . Wir sollen uns nicht mühen

um andre Namen. Ein für alle Male
ists Orpheus, wenn es singt. Er kommt und geht.
Ists nicht schon viel, wenn er die Rosenschale
um ein paar Tage manchmal übersteht?

O . . . wie er schwinden muß, daß ihrs begrifft!

The quotation is from the first section of the cycle and it is
significant that in the second even Orpheus has almost dis-
appeared, as before him God and the Angel, in its celebration of
life in terms of the most abstract and elemental 'image' of breath
itself. Not that there is any lack of 'concrete' force in poems such
as the opening one quoted. Not only is there the characteristic

virtuosity of emphatic assonance – 'Immerfort um das eigne /
Sein rein eingetauschter Weltraum' – but Rilke emphasises the
personal poetic experience by reversing the metaphorical roles:
'Atmen, du unsichtbares Gedicht', rather than the 'orthodox'
comparison of art with nature, and 'Einzige Welle, deren / allmähliches Meer ich bin' where one might expect the more normal
imagery of the ocean of living, the wave of individual existence.
If the poem suggests a rhythmical pattern of existence, it is by
boundlessly extending the poetic experience. The fact that the
poem communicates its belief with such force owes most to that
compelling development of imagery characteristic of Rilke at the
height of his achievement. In the closing lines, emphasising once
more the poetic and personal-calligraphic evidence for the rounded
rhythm of life, the air itself is a once-smooth tree-trunk bearing
the inscription of the poet: 'Du einmal glatte Rinde, / Rundung
und Blatt meiner Worte.'

In the end the Duino Elegies are elegiac in the double sense in
which the term refers to both the matter and the form and it does
seem as if Rilke, in all his involved paradoxes of presence and
absence and in all his counsels of submitting to loss and transformation is ringing the changes on the theme of 'Umschlag' in
art itself, which fills the air with music and in which that 'emptiness' vibrates into melody, like the melody of the lament for
Linos, which is the final point of reference in the First Elegy:

Ist die Sage umsonst, daß einst in der Klage um Linos
wagende erste Musik dürre Erstarrung durchdrang;
daß erst im erschrockenen Raum, dem ein beinah göttlicher
                                       Jüngling
plötzlich für immer enttrat, das Leere in jene
Schwingung geriet, die uns jetzt hinreißst und tröstet und hilft.

This would seem to be the centre of reference for the Elegies
generally as well as for that particular earlier passage in the First
Elegy on the 'emptiness' that is nevertheless an intensification
and expansion of the 'spaces we breathe'. It is admittedly an affirmation in terms of the birth of music out of the spirit of tragedy, and
its mythical expression has, moreover, a kind of conceptual bare-

ness very different to the mythological richness of Hölderlin's
'Vater Äther'. To that extent it would seem to be a very inward looking experience of art as its own myth. The 'argument' of Rilke's
poetry might seem to lead to a Nietzschean formalism, or even,
in its many variations on the theme of totality, as in the sonnet:
'Brau uns den Zauber, in dem die Grenzen sich lösen, / immer
zum Feuer gebeugter Geist! / Diese, vor allem, heimliche Grenze
des Bösen . . .'[96], to echo Nietzsche's 'grandiose indifference' of an
amoral life-principle. Yet any such abstracted argument is patently
at variance with the spirit of the poetry, whose vocabulary of
'piety' could hardly contrast more sharply with Benn's vocabulary
of 'provocation' or Nietzsche's vocabulary of 'malice'. There is
little suggestion in Rilke that art is 'perverse' or a counter-force.

4 *Wo ich schaffe, bin ich wahr*

Perhaps the most famous line in Rilke is the closing line of the Requiem for Wolf Graf von Kalckreuth: [97]

Wer spricht von Siegen? Überstehn ist alles.

The line is often quoted and in many contexts, but in the poem itself the reference is to the artistic 'Umschlag' as the way of withstanding. Had the poet waited, he would have experienced how 'destiny disappears', is transfigured into its image:

. . .

Was hast du nicht gewartet, daß die Schwere
ganz unerträglich wird: da schlägt sie um
und ist so schwer, weil sie so echt ist.

. . .

Dies war die Rettung, hättest du nur ein Mal
gesehn, wie Schicksal in die Verse eingeht
und nicht zurückkommt, wie es drinnen Bild wird
und nichts als Bild . . .
du hättest ausgeharrt.

The self-healing, self-fulfilment of the artist is the aspect most stressed in Rilke's earlier reflections on art, as in the Florentine Diary: 'Wisset denn, daß die Kunst ist: das Mittel Einzelner, Einsamer, sich selbst zu erfüllen.' 'Wisset denn, daß der Künstler für sich schafft – einzig für sich'.[98] The work of art, anonymous with regard to the outside world, turns a personal aspect to the artist as the proof of himself: 'Darin liegt die ungeheure Hilfe des Kunstdings für das Leben dessen, der es machen muß: daß es seine Zusammenfassung ist . . . der Beweis . . . seiner Einheit und Wahrhaftigkeit, der doch nur ihm selber sich zugekehrt und nach außen anonym wirkt. . . .'[99] Reflections of this kind are most frequent in Rilke's letters at the time he was writing *Die Aufzeichnungen des Malte Laurids Brigge* and it is the most central work in this connection, both as a parable of artistic self-healing and by virtue of its position in Rilke's life. According to von Salis, Rilke objected to biographical interpretations of *Malte*, but this must be understood in conjunction with Rilke's own comment: 'Seine Jugend war die meine. Die vielen Leiden, die wir zusammen durchgemacht hatten, hatte ich langsam auf ihn abgeladen. Dies hatte mich . . . von ihm entfernt.'[100] For Malte, too, 'Mamans kleine Sophie', 'Angst' has its origin in a fatefully make-believe childhood and takes the form of being known, of every kind of 'fame'. Towards the end of his story, Malte is beginning to realise the necessity of being nobody's son, to learn the 'true' meaning of the parable of the prodigal son, driven forth by the love he feared and setting out to learn the open and anonymous love of being: 'Das war die Zeit, die damit begann, daß er sich allgemein und anonym fühlte wie ein zögernd Genesender. Er liebte nicht, es sei denn, daß er es liebte zu sein.'[101] But for Malte, as Rilke often emphasises, there is no redemption. 'Freuen Sie sich übrigens nicht zu sehr auf ihn; Sie wissen, er geht an eben dieser "Hölle" zugrunde und endgültig, ohne Pardon noch Auferstehung.'[102] Whenever Rilke speaks of the work in his letters, it is usually in terms of Malte's downfall, and to remind his readers that the work can only be understood if it is read 'gegen den Strom' – 'Daß der arme Malte daran zugrunde geht, ist seine Sache. . . .'[103] It may be that Rilke so often stresses the downfall of Malte because this, in the work itself, is less evident and less an event than a negative matter of a purpose that remains unfulfilled. Malte's questioning reflections on life, in the long passage at the beginning of the book that forms the basis for all that follows, ends with the answer: 'Dieser junge belanglose Ausländer, Brigge, wird sich fünf Treppen hoch hinsetzen müssen und schreiben Tag und Nacht: Ja, er wird schreiben müssen, das wird das Ende sein.'[104] But Malte is unable to take the step towards the 'blessedness' of artistic creativity, of which

Rilke said that for himself he wished 'keine andere Seligkeit': 'Nur ein Schritt, und mein tiefes Elend würde Seligkeit sein. Aber ich kann diesen Schritt nicht tun. . . .'[105]

These variations on the theme of the artist's own 'Rettung', 'Erlösung', 'Seligkeit', are only unusual in being so very insistent and absolutist. But Rilke repeatedly considers the significance of the manner in which art transforms the whole of life, including that which materially is apparently amorphous or 'heavy'. The accent is on the 'whole', for what Rilke stresses most is art's 'Vollzähligkeit'. This does not primarily refer to the totality of the work of art in itself, but rather to the fact that its material is the whole of life. Art is not selective: 'Die Kunst nicht für eine *Auswahl* aus der Welt zu halten, sondern für deren restlose Verwandlung ins Herrliche hinein. . . . Es kann im Schrecklichen nichts so Absagendes und Verneinendes geben, daß nicht die multiple Aktion künstlerischer Bewältigung es mit einem großen, positiven Überschuß zurückließe, als ein Dasein-Aussagendes, Sein-Wollendes: als einen Engel.'[106] The theme is constant throughout Rilke's letters and usually takes the form either of an absolute and exclusive claim for art: '. . . denn in der Kunst ist wirklich Raum für alle Gegensätzlichkeiten der inneren Verhältnisse, nur in ihr . . .', or of attitudes to life in terms of art-analogy: '. . . etwa wie im Kunstwerk das Schwere, ja selbst das Häßliche über dem reinen Dasein, das es annimmt, sich nur noch als Stärke, als Entschlossenheit und Fülle des Lebens offenbart.' '. . . Und über das gründliche Miterlebnis des Todes: verhält es sich damit nicht, wie mit dem Häßlichen in der Kunst, das eben durch die Bewältigung zur Kunst schuldlos wird?'[107] Writing of Strindberg he remarks that the lay reader would be shocked by the cruel elements, but the artist would experience once more how the work of art transforms the most terrible into 'pure intensity' and thus into 'blessedness'.[108] 'Holiness' begins with the realisation that to reject anything is a fall from grace and whoever has failed to reach this state of total affirmation may in Heaven see the Blessed Virgin and the lesser prophets, but not Cézanne and not God.[109] Compared with the catholicism even of the Catholic Church, art has 'die überaus größere . . . Lebensperipherie'.[110]

Without over-systematising those and many similar statements, they do seem to underline that Rilke's most basic and deepest-rooted objection to Christianity is its worship of an 'impious' and 'correcting' God. Often he contrasts the 'natural' faith of the Jews, of the Old Testament, with the forced artificiality of the New Testament, which has fallen into moralising distinctions, foreign to the spontaneous believer.[111] More generally, he accuses all organised religions of betraying the ideal of totality in offering the limited refuge of a partial security. The only valid security is in the 'insecurity' of the whole, but men have always looked for some more definitive refuge and hence, says Rilke, are so strange to him, to whom art has given the experience of 'a profounder, not moral, scarcely even human equilibrium'. Our security, he declares with finality, must relate to the whole, recognising the 'innocence of injustice' and the 'formality of suffering', must reject all names and suspect nothing, must, in short, be 'infinite security in infinite insecurity'.

> Unsere Sicherheit muß irgendwie ein Verhältnis zum Ganzen werden, zu einer Vollzähligkeit; Sichersein heißt für uns die Unschuld des Unrechts gewahren und die Gestalthaftigkeit des Leidens zugeben; heißt Namen ablehnen . . . heißt nichts verdächtigen . . . heißt über allen Begriff des Eigentums hinaus in Aneignungen zu leben, nicht in besitzenden, aber in gleichnishaften. . . . Die Unsicherheit ganz groß nehmen – : in einer unendlichen wird auch die Sicherheit unendlich. . . .[112]

Men are unhappy and guilty because they have broken loose from the whole, insist on using names where there should be none. The ideal man would have the harmonious completion of Nature, in whom the most terrible or cruel is an expression of innocent totality. Rilke rarely formulates quite so uncompromisingly, but there are echoes of the same idea in many letters.[113]

The guiding principle of 'Vollzähligkeit' involves, then, the affirmation not only of an 'uninterrupted' world of life and death, but also an 'uncorrected' world. In a letter to Pongs Rilke expressly rejects the notion of a world that must be 'korrigiert' and

c

declares his faith in a 'Gott der Vollzähligkeit'.[114] In the particular context much of what he says is certainly prompted by his mistrust of any 'socialist' measures. It is most of all this letter, as containing 'the kernel of Rilke's social teaching', that is used in evidence against Rilke by Egon Schwarz, evidence for Rilke's 'Absage an jede Veränderung der Gesellschaft', for his confusion of social circumstances with 'nature', for what, in the opinion of the critic, is the spurious message of the spiritual values of god-given human misery, which Rilke shares with the Christian tradition, though distinguished from it otherwise by his radically individualistic solipsism.[115] Criticism on the political front can be only too well documented from Rilke's letters. Apart from the Pongs letter, there are above all the notorious 'lettres milanaises', most usually cited in evidence of Rilke's flirtation with fascism, the letters to his young Milanese admirer, the Duchess Gallarati-Scotti. Even if one is not primarily concerned with Rilke's politics, there does seem, merely in the light of his letter writing generally, particular reason for regarding these letters as unusually indicative of Rilke's sentiments. Most readers of Rilke's letters are struck by the way in which they are so delicately modulated in sympathy with the different recipients, whereas here Rilke obstinately insists on opinions opposed to those of the Duchess herself. 'Non, cher Rilke, je ne suis pas une admiratrice de M. Mussolini . . . Il serait trop long de vous dire toutes les raisons que dès le commencement m'ont rendu impossible une adhésion quelconque au fascisme; je vous dirai seulement que pour mon compte je déteste la violence, et je la supporte encore moins quand elle agit en ma faveur ou en faveur de ma classe sociale que si elle est adoptée par mes ennemis. En second lieu je pense que la tranquillité d'un pays est seulement assurée lorsque la liberté permet d'avoir une idée exacte de ce que pense et veut le pays, – au moins un minimum de liberté, ce qui est du reste le premier droit apporté par la civilisation.'[116]

It is ironic that it is in these, his most political letters, that Rilke most protests his unconcern with politics. 'En politique, je n'ai aucune voix, aucune – et je me défends d'y engager aucun sentiment.' Ironic but not contradictory, for it is in distancing himself from the political sphere that his own political views emerge. In the course of his reply to the letter quoted, he says once more: 'Quant à la politique, je suis si loin d'elle, si incapable de suivre et de m'expliquer ses mouvements et ses contrecoups que ce serait ridicule de vouloir me prononcer sur n'importe quel événement situé dans son domaine. . . .' Inevitably, 'pronouncements' are the follow-up on this disclaimer. On the one hand: 'La liberté! Mais n'est-ce point d'elle que le monde est malade? . . .', or: '. . . ce parlamentarisme vide et vaniteux. . . .' On the other hand – and it is a disturbing link between his 'totality' and totalitarianism – he defends, expressly by way of analogy with the innocent cruelty of nature and of art, 'les veritables dictateurs . . . en exerçant une salutaire et sûre violence. . . .' The Duchess flatly rejects his reading of history, but for Rilke it is a case of 'heureuse Italie!' and with some embarrassment one reads how this so pacifist and internationalist poet might imagine himself to be 'avec conviction et enthusiasme . . . soldat italien, soldat français, oui . . . jusqu'à l'extrême sacrifice'.[117]

It is hardly necessary to list the items of ammunition supplied by Rilke, not only in these letters but in many others and in his work generally, to critics attacking him in the social and political context, items familiar from that persistent German pattern of culture versus civilisation – Slavonic soulfulness as against the rationalism that threatens Germany from the West, the distrust and daemonisation of the city as against the romantic transfiguration of the country, the particular insistence in the case of Rilke on the solitariness of art and his generally negative attitude towards the public and the democratic, towards the media and the 'jüdische Spitzfindigkeit' of the press. Not that Rilke would be vulgarly anti-semitic, rather it is a case of praising the great tradition of the biblical Jews in a manner that devalues the present day and the Jews of the present day.[118] To some of this, as to the mere mention of the German Master, Dürer, Schwarz may be over allergic, but it is noteworthy that, in his general analysis, Schwarz is in effect putting forward a view of Rilke not unlike that of Mason, as when he suggests 'die innerliche Ausbildung des Individuums' as Rilke's highest value. Only Schwarz is concerned

with other matters and he very compellingly relates this view of
Rilke to the political and social matters with which he is concerned.

> Rilke's größter Fehler im Zeitalter der Massenbewegungen und
> kollektiven Probleme war vor allem ein extremer Individualis-
> mus, der ihm den Blick auf die eigentlichen Bewegkräfte der
> Epoche verbaute. Die Nation reagiert für ihn wie ein einzelner
> Mensch . . . die Armen bilden nicht etwa eine einheitliche
> Gruppe, die ihren Zustand gemeinsamen Ursachen verdankt,
> sondern jeder ist elend für sich allein und auf seine besondere
> Weise. Daher blieb Rilke blind für die großen Mächte seiner
> Zeit, die das Individuum zwingen und überwältigen. Kurz, er
> hatte wenig historischen Sinn und verstand im Grunde nicht,
> was sich in seiner Umwelt wirklich abspielte. Seine Stärke lag
> im Seelischen.[119]

Schwarz would see all of this related to and reflected in Rilke's
work. He suggests that the 'teaching' of the transformation into
invisibility in the Duino Elegies is 'poetisch und politisch gesprochen, das Kernstück der Rilkeschen Weltanschauung' and
comments on the famous passage on man's mission 'zu sagen:
Haus, Brücke, Brunnen, Tor . . .': 'Dieser vielbewunderte Katalog,
so erhaben und ehrwürdig er sein mag, ist im Grunde nichts als
Flucht in eine vorkapitalistische Vergangenheit, ist Blut und Boden.
Sofern er sich auch für ein Zukunftsprogramm hält, entbehrt er,
wie wir heute mit dem Schauder der Erfahrung sagen können,
keineswegs einer atavistischen, schreckenerregenden Kompon-
ente.'[120] This is a harsh formulation, but much the same has been
urged against Rilke's mythology by Peter Demetz, who would be
prepared to shrug off more lightly Rilke's opinions on public
affairs.[121] In effect Schwarz would see the Duino Elegies and the
'lettres milanaises' as two sides of the same coin, in spirit if not
in form 'Zwillingserscheinungen', the one 'Geschichtsmythos', the
other 'Geschichtstheorie'. Even without evading this argument by
appealing to poetic values independent of any message, one may
feel that the message itself cannot be so summarily dismissed
unless one adopts an extreme position, recognising only social and

political categories and declaring the more metaphysical mysteries of life and death, good and evil, to be non-issues. Yet one's approach to Rilke can be quite different and one will still come up against the questions raised by Schwarz and in particular perhaps critics of all shades come up against that concept of 'Vollzählig-keit', of which Schwarz, laying his own particular emphasis, suggests that it allowed Rilke to tolerate the most terrible social evils. If Schwarz takes exception especially to poems like the Orphic sonnet on hunting, with its italicised affirmation: 'Töten ist eine Gestalt unseres wandernden Trauerns', he is seeing Rilke in a particular context, in the tradition of what he calls the 'Totenkult der europäischen Rechten'.[122] But it is noteworthy that critics as sympathetic as Peters and Leishman cite the same poem as an example of those aspects of Rilke's thinking they find impossible to accept. Ronald Gray speaks of Rilke's 'mysticism' as being of the 'natural' rather than of the theistic kind, of a kind that is indifferent to distinctions of good and evil.[123] While Rilke himself would shy away from the term 'godless' that Gray applies to his beliefs, Rilke's 'Gott der Vollzähligkeit', in so far as it can be regarded in any sense as a theological definition, is doubtless uncompromisingly unchristian. However, Rilke hardly adopts a consistent standpoint. While he often equates the God of Totality with the God of the Old Testament, at other times he suggests that a 'blind fate' – the phrase seems modified by Rilke's use of quotation marks – is the precondition of being 'innocently alone' and at one with the world.[124]

How Rilke comes to the theme of 'Vollzähligkeit' is clear enough. When, with the prospect of military service at the beginning of the war, he was faced with a repetition of his earlier misery in the military academy, this, he said, was to him un-bearable, for what had he meanwhile done but transform his past experience into art and so affirm it? Now he must experience once more that the reality was nothing but ugly, nothing but senseless – 'daß es kleines, unmögliches Elend war, sonst nichts. . . .'[125] The illogicality, if it is that, is less relevant than the artistic ex-perience that prompted Rilke again and again to ask if there is not a similar point of vantage in the human heart from which all can

be affirmed. Speaking of the sense of totality in Rembrandt's
'Blinding of Samson', he asks once more if in life something
similar can be achieved and ends with a wish to return to his
own work, in which he had always experienced this wholeness:
'Was ist das? Gibt es im Leben ähnliches? gibt es Herzverhält-
nisse, die das Grausamste einschließen, um der Vollzähligkeit
willen, weil die Welt doch erst Welt ist, wenn A l l e s darin
geschieht; ich konnte mir Gott immer nur als Den denken, der
a l l e s zuläßt . . . Darum sehne ich mich so nach meiner
Arbeit, weil mir von ihr aus immer alles recht war; da war nie
ein Schreckliches zu erleben, ohne daß ein Engel aus dem Gegenteil
neben einen trat und mit hineinsah.'[126] He cherished the belief
that this ideal is attainable in 'real life' too, so that art would be
in the true sense, not only for him but for others, a way of living
life. The idea is expressed with particular insistence in the letters
to Merline. One should not attach oneself to details, but recog-
nise the validity of 'le tout'. Once more he is deriving his 'Lebenshaltung' – to use a term more appropriate to Rilke than 'Weltanschauung' – from art and he expressly points out the parallel:
'Pensez, mon amie, au dyptique du roi André que nous avons
admiré au Musée: même ces pierres grises et tristes, même ces
perles percées de leur clou d'or contribuent à la splendeur génér-
ale.'[127] Such a response to art is the invariable criterion where
Rilke philosophises on life and in that sense 'das Künstlerdasein'
is the main subject and the starting-point for those affirmations of
'being' that, as critics generally agree, dominate especially in
the later poetry with their 'consent à lui-même', 'consent à être'.
Rilke criticism is less unanimous when it comes to distinguishing
the nature of that affirmation, and it is perhaps better, as it is
certainly less controversial, to stress its source. In particular, the
'grace' of that miracle of inspiration in 1922 seemed to him
'mehr als nur ein privates Ereignis zu sein, denn es ist damit ein
Maß gegeben für die unerschöpfliche Schichtung unserer Natur.'[128]
It is an axiom of the artistic experience as Rilke speaks of it, that
the very nature of poetry is felt to be mysteriously affirmative, just
as he says of rhyme: 'C'est une très grande déesse, la divinité de
coincidences très secrètes et très anciennes . . . évoquée, mais

jamais cherchée. . . . La vraie rime n'est pas un moyen de la poésie, c'est un "oui" infiniment affirmatif.'[129]

The emphasis on secrecy and mystery is characteristic, to the extent even that knowledge is suspect, though one probably should not labour the anti-rationalism of this attitude. 'Das Geheimnis des Daseins ruht nicht im Wissen'. Terms like 'unbewußt' and 'jungfräulich' recur frequently when he speaks of artistic creativity. When he is at work, he says of his own poetic practice, no one, not even himself, may 'look on'. To read criticism of his own work would be the kind of 'acrobatics' the artist must avoid, who must rather, like Cézanne, remain at the centre of his occupation.[130] Van Gogh's letters, by contrast, are all too readable: 'Der Maler dürfte nicht zum Bewusstsein seiner Einsichten kommen (wie der Künstler überhaupt).' The solitary Beethoven is held up as an example, who with his deafness was no longer 'opposite' his work.[131] In Rilke's poetry the distrust of knowledge appears as an aversion to 'names', a recurring theme in his work up to the 'namelessness' of his epitaph. Often the suggestion is conveyed that life only remains pure because none can know it, that if it were wholly possible to man, it would not only be humanly limited, but above all 'getrübt'. A characteristic of Rilke's vocabulary is the frequently positive purpose of words formed with 'Nicht-' and 'Un-': the motifs of 'Nicht-Wissen' and 'Un-Möglichkeit'. What inwardly is anonymously 'heil' is ever and again contrasted with the outer, inquisitive and destructive names. 'Was draußen heißt, ist lauter Heilung innen,' he writes to Erika Mitterer, and for Merline he writes the poem 'Die Innenansicht'[132]

wie war in dir, mein stiller Schooß,
alles trotzdem namenlos:
draußen erst heißen die Dinge.

Heißen nach Zweifel und heißen nach Zeit. . . .

One must be very cautious with names, he writes to Kappus in one of his more questionable variations on the theme, for it is so often the name of a crime which destroys life, rather than the nameless and conciliatory act itself. Not only in the correspondence with Kappus, but in so many other letters of counselling, this 'Anonym-Nehmen' is often the substance of his advice.[133] At the same time the motif of mystery and 'Nicht-Wissen' in Rilke carries with it the suggestion of initiation and that 'Fast-es-schon-wissen', from which he claims to derive a sense of security even at the lowest points of his creative life. So he writes towards the end of 1921. 'Zeit und Alter sind mir immer weniger wesentlich geworden . . . und selbst Leben und Tod! Wie offen die Wege von einem zum andern für uns, wie nahe, wie nah am Fast-es-schon-wissen, wie fast schon Wort dieses dieses, in dem sie zur (vorläufig namenlosen) Einheit zusammenstürzen. Dies also ängstigt mich nicht. . . .' The inner indestructibility of all truly experienced existence, 'dieses unbeschreibliche Bleiben', of which he speaks in his letters, is something which he believed he had known in moments of 'mystical' insight and he recorded those strange experiences of integration into an 'unbroken' world in several autobiographical fragments.[134] But these descriptions, his letters suggest, were pale reflections of what were 'Annäherungen an die Grenzempfindungen des Daseins'. Such 'weltisches Teilnehmen' was rather to be communicated by way of symbols, like the bird-flight and the bird-song that are recurring themes in his poetry and of which he writes in the letters to Lou Andreas-Salomé: '. . . darum fassen wir einen Vogellaut so leicht ins Innere auf . . . er kann uns für einen Augenblick die ganze Welt zum Innenraum machen, weil wir fühlen, daß der Vogel nicht unterscheidet zwischen seinem Herzen und dem ihren.' Here too he speaks of the 'openly-mysterious', of the mysteries of religions and of nature itself that are nowhere hidden and uncertain, but open secrets: 'Das, was da so schön von der Pflanzenwelt gezeigt wird, wie sie kein Geheimnis macht aus ihrem Geheimnis, wissend gleichsam, daß es anders nicht a l s i n S i c h e r h e i t sein könne: das ist, denk Dir, was ich in Ägypten vor den Skulpturen empfand . . . dieses Bloßgelegtsein des Geheimnisses, das so durch und durch, so an jeder Stelle geheim ist, daß man es nicht zu verstecken braucht.'[135]

'Unser ist: den Ausgang nicht zu wissen . . . ,' says Rilke in the poem 'An den Engel', and in the letters he repeatedly counsels accepting the mysterious as such, expressing his own distaste for the inquisitive and impatient. 'Im Übrigen gehört es zu den ursprünglichen Neigungen meiner Anlage, das Geheime a l s s o l c h e s aufzunehmen, nicht als ein zu Entlarvendes, sondern als das Geheimnis, das *so* bis in sein Innerstes, und überall, geheim ist, wie ein Stück Zucker an jeder Stelle Zucker ist. . . . Wieviele Früchte, die für uns gemeint waren . . . haben neugierige Geister im Reifen unterbrochen.'[136] 'Man weiß Gott sei Dank den Sinn des Lebens nicht,' said Rilke towards the end of his life, in 1924, and the artist above all should need no other enlightenment than the proof of his profession: '. . . denn am Ende überwiegt in diesem wunderlichsten Berufe die bénédiction.' What the poet experiences is the 'healing figure', the form for the question, and if he offers an answer it is by communicating that experience. 'Des Künstlers ist es, das Rätsel zu – lieben,' says Rilke in *Worpswede*.[137]

5 *Ce céleste retour*: the mission of art

In spite of these many agnostic professions, the Duino Elegies themselves are more specific, in suggesting the mission of man's artistic 'Auftrag', and it is the aspect of the Elegies central to Rilke's own most considerable commentary, the famous letter to his Polish translator Hulewicz on the 'great unity' of existence and on the function of man to remain so open to and absorbent of life as to transform the transitory and visible into an invisible and abiding inwardness.[138] In the Ninth Elegy, in its opening restatement of the sense of exclusion and transitoriness, the theme is first questioningly and tentatively introduced: 'Sind wir vielleicht h i e r, um zu sagen: Haus / Brücke, Brunnen, Tor, Krug, Obstbaum, Fenster, – / höchstens: Säule, Turm . . . aber zu s a g e n, verstehs, oh zu sagen s o, wie selber die Dinge niemals / innig meinten zu sein.' The theme is fully developed in the closing passages: 'Preise dem Engel die Welt. . . . . Sag ihm die Dinge. . . .' This is the climax of the cycle and here, too, one can justly speak of the clarity of the Elegies, provided one accepts that this means clear, not only in whatever certainties they imply, certainties of enrichment and fulfilment, but also clear in their uncertainties – 'wer wir am Ende auch seien'.

> . . . Und diese, von Hingang
> lebenden Dinge verstehn, daß du sie rühmst;
> vergänglich,
> traun sie ein Rettendes uns, den Vergänglichsten zu.
> Wollen, wir sollen sie ganz im unsichtbarn Herzen
> verwandeln

in – o unendlich – in uns! Wer wir am Ende auch seien.
Erde, ist es nicht dies, was du willst: u n s i c h t b a r
in uns erstehn? – Ist es dein Traum nicht,
einmal unsichtbar zu sein? – Erde! unsichtbar!
Was, wenn Verwandlung nicht, ist dein drängender
                                              Auftrag?
Erde, du liebe, ich will! Oh glaub, es bedürfte
nicht deiner Frühlinge mehr, mich dir zu gewinnen –
                                      e i n e r,
ach, ein einziger ist schon dem Blute zu viel.
Namenlos bin ich zu dir entschlossen, von weit her.
Immer warst du im Recht, und dein heiliger Einfall
ist der vertrauliche Tod.

Siehe, ich lebe. Woraus? Weder Kindheit noch Zukunft
werden weniger. . . . Überzähliges Dasein
entspringt mir im Herzen.

Nothing links Rilke more clearly to the German Romantic tradition than his motif or myth of language itself, of its creative
power to establish what 'remains', as in the famous phrase of
Hölderlin: 'Was bleibet aber / Stiften die Dichter.' There are
links of many kinds, most obviously perhaps with Novalis. Many
of the passages quoted earlier on the open-secrecy of life seem to
echo Novalis' 'Das große Geheimnis ist allen offenbart und
bleibt ewig unergründlich.' The echoes would serve to emphasise
the darker and more irrational elements that anti-romantic
criticism might find in Rilke – such echoes of Novalis as the
tragic origin of art itself: 'Die Dichtung sang's dem traurigen
Bedarfe,' or a certain tragic epistemology that, Kleistian fashion,
emphasises the fall of man out of unknowing nature. 'Seine
Begierde, Gott zu werden, hat ihn von uns getrennt, er sucht was
wir nicht wissen und ahnden können . . .,' says Nature in *Die
Lehrlinge zu Sais* and one motif in *Heinrich von Ofterdingen* is the
contrast between the 'sounding tree of life' and the 'tree of knowledge and war'. Or again for those other passages of Rilke on the
danger of naming and numbering it is easy to find parallels

even with the same suggestion of an ideal of lawless totality, for example in the Hymns: [139]

> Verschwunden waren die Götter,
> Einsam und leblos
> Stand die Natur,
> Entseelt von der strengen Zahl
> Und der eisernen Kette.
> Gesetze wurden.
> Und in Begriffe,
> Wie in Staub und Lüfte,
> Zerfiel die unermeßliche Blüte
> Des tausendfachen Lebens.

Yet one feels that the echoes in Rilke recall more than they re-create the Romantic world. In the abstract one might say that the mediating role of man in Rilke is much as in the lines from Hölderlin's *Der Rhein*: '. . . weil die Seeligsten nichts fühlen von selbst . . . muß in der Götter Nahmen / Theilnehmend fühlen ein Andrer.' But just as the Orpheus motif of the breathing life of art recalls both Novalis and Hölderlin and yet has an abstract remoteness and lonely self-centredness very different to the animistic imagery of Novalis or Hölderlin's Vater-Äther myth, so too it is questionable if in general Rilke communicates the same faith or feeling of faith as do the Romantics themselves. Lawrence Ryan characterises Rilke as 'Romantiker in dürftiger Zeit', failing to find in his poetry the true Romantic 'Sprachwerdung des Seins'.[140] But then, in that strange way in which the science of philology is at the very centre of German Romanticism, Romantic mythology, especially the myth of language, seems to belong with the Romantics' discovery of the miracle and mystery of languages and to share the enthusiasm conveyed by their very manner of speaking, as when Schlegel speaks of Plato's 'beautiful Sanskrit'. Read against the background of the original German Romanticism, the presence of the 'Weltseele' does not animate Rilke's world in the same way and Rilke's poetry seems to suggest a lonelier kind of 'Ich-Philosophie'.

It may be partly for reasons like this that the 'Auftrag', for all

that Rilke so much emphasises it himself, is not an aspect of
the Elegies that has greatly appealed to many critics. 'This
development of the theme of invisibility at the end of the ninth
elegy, says Stahl, 'has met with the greatest amount of incom-
prehension and disapproval from Rilke critics.'[141] As already
noted, Schwarz rejects such an unpolitical myth of inwardness,
though one could equally argue that its function in Rilke's poetry
is to find a purposeful direction beyond aesthetic self-containment and contentment with the work of art as an end in itself.
But the 'Auftrag' is no less deplored by Bassermann, as if Rilke
had failed to sustain the more elegiac note. In effect the question
as posed in the opening elegy: 'ach, wen vermögen / wir denn zu
brauchen?' is answered in those later elegies by the earth's need
of man – 'Aber weil Hiersein viel ist, und weil uns scheinbar /
alles das Hiesige braucht' – who has not failed to make use of the
space of existence: 'so haben wir dennoch / nicht die Räume
versäumt.' Bassermann would seem to imply that this is a facile
reversal of roles, but then the whole cycle is seen by Rilke himself in the context of that 'Jubel und Ruhm' expressed in the
opening lines of the Tenth Elegy – and from the reader's point
of view depends, perhaps, on accepting this as a sufficient context. In those letters in 1922 announcing the completion of the
Elegies, Rilke recalls the lines written in 1912:

Daß ich dereinst, an dem Ausgang der grimmigen Einsicht,
Jubel und Ruhm aufsinge zustimmenden Engeln.
Daß von den klargeschlagenen Hämmern des Herzens
keiner versage an weichen, zweifelnden oder
reißenden Saiten. Daß mich mein strömendes Antlitz
glänzender mache: daß das unscheinbare Weinen
blühe. O wie werdet ihr dann, Nächte, mir lieb sein,
gehärmte. Daß ich euch knieender nicht, untröstliche
                                                    Schwestern,
hinnahm, nicht in euer gelöstes
Haar mich gelöster ergab. Wir, Vergeuder der Schmerzen.
Wie wir sie absehn voraus, in die traurige Dauer,
ob sie nicht enden vielleicht, Sie aber sind ja

unser winterwähriges Laub, unser dunkeles Sinngrün,
e i n e der Zeiten des heimlichen Jahres –, nicht nur
Zeit –, sind Stelle, Siedelung, Lager, Boden, Wohnort.

Although Rilke invariably speaks of this experience of elegiac
'meaningfulness' ('unser dunkeles Sinngrün'), not as something
new but as confirmation of his oldest beliefs and prejudices, it is
communicated with a quite new spontaneity in the post-elegiac
poetry, for example in the following poem, which may be regarded as part of the paralipomena to the Orpheus cycle: [142]

Wann war ein Mensch je so wach
wie der Morgen von heut?
nicht nur Blume und Bach
auch das Dach ist erfreut.

Selbst sein alternder Rand,
von den Himmeln erhellt, –
wird fühlend: ist Land,
ist Antwort, ist Welt.

Alles atmet und dankt.
O ihr Nöte der Nacht
wie ihr spurlos versankt.

Aus Scharen von Licht
war ihr Dunkel gemacht,
das sich rein widerspricht.

Rilke might have written this at any period so far as the idea of
the poem is concerned. Attitudes of affirmation are the most obvious constant throughout, even in his period of deepest depression during the war years: 'Und da bekenne ich denn . . . daß
ich das Leben für ein Ding von der unantastbarsten Köstlichkeit
halte, und daß die Verknotung so vieler Verhängnisse und Entsetz-
lichkeiten . . . mich nicht irre machen kann an der Fülle und
Güte und Zugeneigtheit des Daseins.' But there is a new impulse
after the 'miraculous' inspiration of the Elegies and Sonnets and
the experience, once for all, of 'Vollzähligkeit'. He writes to his

daughter: 'Vergiß es nie, daß Du reich bist, ich sage: b i s t, ein für allemal . . . die meisten Menschen . . . nehmen schief und verlieren dabei.' He begins to review his earlier work and to see as its moral a boundless affirmation, in its very concern with dark themes a tribute to the whole of life. In March 1922 he writes:

> Jenes 'Schwer-Nehmen' des Lebens, von dem meine Bücher erfüllt sind –, ist ja keine Schwermütigkeit . . . jenes Schwer-nehmen will ja nichts sein, nicht wahr?, als ein Nehmen nach dem wahren Gewicht, also ein Wahr-nehmen; ein Versuch, die Dinge mit dem Karat des Herzens zu wägen, statt mit Verdacht, Glück oder Zufall. Keine Absage, nicht wahr?! K e i n e A b s a g e ; oh, im Gegenteil, wieviel unendliche Zustimmung und immer noch Zustimmung zum Da-Sein!

If the spontaneity diminishes in the last years, he holds fast to the belief that his work bears witness to the 'innocence' of all life and is quick to welcome any sign that it had been so understood.[143]

'Alles atmet und dankt. . . .' The breath of life motif is one of the most dominant in the post-elegiac poetry. One of his last compositions is the trilogy 'O Lacrimosa': [144]

> Nichts als ein Atemzug ist das Leere, und jenes
> grüne Gefülltsein der schönen
> Bäume: ein Atemzug!
> Wir, die Angeatmeten noch,
> heute noch Angeatmeten, zählen
> diese, der Erde, langsame Atmung,
> deren Eile wir sind.

A characteristic of the latest work is its 'earthliness' and there is a new note of acceptance and even equanimity with respect to the theme of death, a theme which is no less evident in the last poems, but on the contrary rather more open and immediate. In the Duino Elegies themselves the attitude towards death is seen as the most significant factor of man's 'Lebenshaltung'. The Fifth Elegy, ending the first half of the cycle, and the concluding Tenth

Elegy both centre on contrasting images of truthful and falsified
landscapes of death. The test of truth is the assimilation of death,
as opposed to the Fifth Elegy's unreal city of Madame Lamort's
fashion world of death-decked-out or the Tenth Elegy's fair-
ground imagery of a spurious deathlessness. The more particular
emphasis in the Fifth Elegy, with its reference both to the
Picasso picture and to the art of the acrobats, is on artistry and
art, whereas the Tenth Elegy widens the scope of reference to a
more general attitude to life, in line with Rilke's practice to
deduce laws of living from the pattern of art-experience. The
Fifth Elegy, in which the travelling acrobats are symbolic of
humanity's transient activity, is a reflection on the precarious
nature of art and the art of living, in which mastery is so rarely
achieved except at the expense of total truth. Following on the
passage of Madame Lamort and in contrast with it, the elegy ends
with the image of an ideal artistic expertise that would retain its
validity *sub specie mortis*:

> Engel!: Es wäre ein Platz, den wir nicht wissen, und dorten,
> auf unsäglichem Teppich, zeigten die Liebenden, die's hier
> bis zum Können nie bringen, ihre kühnen
> hohen Figuren des Herzschwungs,
> ihre Türme aus Lust, ihre
> längst, wo Boden nie war, nur an einander
> lehnenden Leitern, bebend, – und k ö n n t e n s,
> vor den Zuschauern rings, unzähligen lautlosen Toten:
> Würfen die dann ihre letzten, immer ersparten,
> immer verborgenen, die wir nicht kennen, ewig
> gültigen Münzen des Glücks vor das endlich
> wahrhaft lächelnde Paar auf gestilltem
> Teppich?

The Tenth Elegy, finally, is specifically the death elegy, with its
conjuration of the Egyptian landscape, as the culture most
centred, with 'desert clarity' as Rilke said to Hulewicz, on death
and as opposed to cultures founded on 'distraction' and 'deathlessness', and brings the whole cycle to a close with paradoxical
symbols of falling fulfilment, echoing the 'flowering grief' of the

opening lines of the Tenth Elegy and appropriate to the whole
work as affirmation in elegy form:

Aber erweckten sie uns, die unendlich Toten, ein Gleichnis,
siehe, sie zeigten vielleicht auf die Kätzchen der leeren
Hasel, die hängenden, oder
meinten den Regen, der fällt auf dunkles Erdreich im Frühjahr. –

Und wir,die an s t e i g e n d e s Glück
denken, empfänden die Rührung,
die uns beinah bestürzt,
wenn ein Glückliches f ä l l t.

In the last poems the reflections on life centre more than ever
before on attitudes towards mourning and death, as in the cycle
of poems *Im Kirchhof zu Ragaz* with its several variations on the
theme of totality: as complete 'communion' in the second poem,
with its metaphorical elaboration of the 'kitchen-arts' of the
dead, or, in the fifth poem, as 'equanimity' (that 'Gleichmut'
associated with death in the Fourth and Tenth Elegies) in the
imagery of the balanced 'scales of death' and the 'unsteady' or
'rarely balanced' scales of life.[145]
In the letters of his last years Rilke rejects any more other-
worldly consolation in the face of death, suggesting, moreover,
that it is rather the concept of a 'Jenseits' that estranges death
and makes the dead more remote. In place of any other dogma
Rilke claims that the heart can encompass the 'pure contradictions' of life in an attitude variously referred to as piety or
totality, anonymity or 'Arglosigkeit'. In a letter on Malte's 'thèse
secrète' we read that whoever accomplishes this love 'imperturb-
ably' knows that: 'le mot "séparation" n'est qu'un nom dénué de
tout sens, à moins que ce soit l'anonymat délicieux d'un nombre
infini de découvertes, d'harmonies inédites et d'inimaginables
pénétrances. . . .'[146] As in his epitaph, the rose is Rilke's symbol
for this unity of 'pure contradiction', and here he says: 'Tous les
jours, en contemplant ces admirables roses blanches, je me
demande si elles ne sont pas l'image la plus parfaite de cette

unité, je dirais même de cette identité d'absence et de présence
qui, peut-être, constitue l'équation fondamentale de notre vie?'
    To draw any dogmatic conclusions from this Rilkean 'absence'
is probably to make the concept less ambiguous than it really is
and perhaps not really so relevant to the poetry, in which it is
rather the attitude that is unambiguous. In the Duino Elegies themselves the Fourth Elegy had ended with an image of the childlike
attitude of 'Arglosigkeit' towards death. Guilt is 'easily divined',
but innocence is a mystery and the innocent attitude of mind is
in the end indescribable, though expressible in the metaphors and
images of art :

> Wer zeigt ein Kind, so wie es steht? Wer stellt
> es ins Gestirn und giebt das Maß des Abstands
> ihm in die Hand? Wer macht den Kindertod
> aus grauem Brot, das hart wird, – oder läßt
> ihn drin im runden Mund, so wie den Gröps
> von einem schönen Apfel? ... Mörder sind
> leicht einzusehen. Aber dies: den Tod,
> den ganzen Tod, noch v o r dem Leben so
> sanft zu enthalten und nicht bös zu sein,
> ist unbeschreiblich.

    Among the poems of Rilke's last years there are several which
are post-elegiac in a special sense. To various friends he sent
copies of the Duino Elegies with dedicatory verses. For example
to Hans Carossa:

> Auch noch Verlieren ist *unser*; und selbst das Vergessen
> hat noch Gestalt in dem bleibenden Reich
> > der Verwandlung.
> Losgelassenes kreist; und sind wir auch selten die Mitte
> einem der Kreise: sie ziehn um uns die heile Figur.

To Hulewicz he sent, as well as the famous commentary, the
verses: [147]

> Glücklich, die wissen, daß hinter allen
> Sprachen das Unsägliche steht;

daß, von dort her, ins Wohlgefallen
Größe zu uns übergeht!

    Unabhängig von diesen Brücken
die wir mit Verschiedenem baun:
so daß wir immer, aus jedem Entzücken
in ein heiter Gemeinsames schaun.

'Heiter Gemeinsames' is a new theme in Rilke and indicative of
a new-found feeling:[148]

Wo sich langsam aus dem Schon-Vergessen
einst Erfahrnes uns entgegenhebt,
rein gemeistert, milde, unermessen
und im Unantastbaren erlebt:

Dort beginnt das Wort, wie wir es meinen;
seine Geltung übertrifft uns still.
Denn der Geist, der uns vereinsamt, will
völlig sicher sein, uns zu vereinen.

These poems, like many others of the same period, celebrate
'Bezug', the experience of relationship to a whole in a partici-
pation that is at once passive: – 'Wir sind nur Mund. Wer singt
das ferne Herz, / das heil inmitten aller Dinge weilt? . . .' – and
active: – 'Mitzuwirken ist nicht Überhebung / an dem unbe-
schreiblichen Bezug. . . .'[149]
    The 'heile Figur' of the dedication for Carossa is central to all
these poems, but those same verses expressly include 'Verlieren'
and 'Vergessen' as essential elements in this 'Reich der Verwandlung'. 'Auch für ihn spielen Tod und Vergehen keine Rolle, so
wenig wie die Zeitfolgen,' says Rehm of the later Rilke, but there
is something unreal about this suggestion, most of all with regard
to Rilke's last years. In the letters of this period there is a
simpler confession of feeling. 'Ah, welche Leichtigkeit des Vogels,
der verspricht, verspricht, zu viel verspricht.'[150] Phrases like this
from his last year, where he is speaking of the first cuckoo of
spring, seem to contrast with the much less direct display of
emotion in his earlier letters.

Rilke does imply a kind of syllogistic certainty. Art shows itself to be intimate with the 'whole', however hostile. Yet art is a human response and therefore man, too, is in the depth of his being, 'vertraut'. Beyond that one can only say that in the latest poetry of Rilke there is an increasingly earthly emphasis: [151]

Die Mandelbäume in Blüte, alles was
wir hier leisten können, ist, sich ohne Rest
erkennen in der irdischen Erscheinung.

There is even, within the myth of an 'infinite' nature, a growing or at any rate more open emphasis on transitoriness. If the Elegies speak of an earthly 'Einmaligkeit' that is 'nicht widerrufbar', it is also 'unwiederbringlich'. When the suggestion was made that Rilke should record some of his poems, he wrote:

. . . Aber freilich, für unsereinen, dem bestimmte Offenbarungen aus ihrer unerhörten Einmaligkeit ihr Unbeschreiblichstes an Größe, Demut und Menschlichkeit zu gewinnen scheinen, wäre ein solches mechanisches Überleben der heimlichsten und reichsten Sprachgewalt fast unerträglich. Noch ist es (neben einer Not) auch eine Stärke und ein Stolz unserer Seele mit dem Einzigen und unwiederbringlich Vergehenden umzugehen.

The quotation is from a letter to Dieter Bassermann and noticeably in the spirit of Bassermann's own Rilke interpretation. Rilke's 'religion' is probably more ambiguous than Bassermann would suggest, but Rilke does, at times, commit himself. As early as 1898 he wrote: 'Wir brauchen die Ewigkeit; denn nur sie gibt unseren Gesten Raum, und doch wissen wir uns in enger Endlichkeit. Wir müssen also innerhalb dieser Schranken eine Unendlichkeit schaffen, da wir an die Grenzlosigkeit nicht mehr glauben.[152] This is untypically explicit, but there is often enough an implicit suggestion of 'tragedy', as well as a suggestion of 'loss' of faith, inevitable when one remembers that Rilke says, speaking in later life of the religious beliefs and practices of his childhood: 'Und alles das hatte noch immer, immer noch Macht über mich.' Elisabeth von Schmidt-Pauli reports the conversation:

' "Glauben Sie denn, Schwester Elisabeth, daß Gott unseretwegen einem Engel befehlen könnte, die Räume zu durchmessen, um uns beizustehen?" ... Da war kein Zögern in mir: "ja – das glaube ich." ... "Dann gibt es für Sie also keine Tragik," sagte er.' Of the ageing Rodin Rilke said that his 'life-mask' had become not less but more tragic – 'tragischer, im Sinne jener antikischen Tragik, in deren Bezirk selbst Götter und Himmel hineinreichen, die sich aber doch zuletzt im Irdischen schloß, als ein Kreis, dessen Wesen und Ewigkeit es ist, aus sich selbst nicht hinauszufinden.' To that extent there is a sense of narcissistic self-imprisonment in the theme of totality and in the Orphic myth of a song-existence that has the perfect self-concentration of the rose: '... niemandem, nirgendshin ... ganz beschäftigt mit dem Genuß des eigenen Gleichgewichts.'[153] The questions that recur throughout the Duino Elegies, questions of 'wer?' and 'wem?', remain unanswered except in the sense that what is on the one hand, especially in the earlier poems, a negative or 'absence', – 'Was ersehnst du der fremden Geliebten verhaltenes Antlitz –, / hat deine Sehnsucht nicht Atem ... oh, so i s t sie auch nicht, nirgends ...' – becomes, especially in the later poems, an anonymous 'presence': [154]

Es liebt ein Herz, daß es die W e l t uns rühme,
nicht sich, nicht den Geliebten, denn: wer wars?
Ein Anonymes preist das Anonyme,
wie Vogelaufruf das Gefühl des Jahrs....

The French poems in particular, with symbols like that of the 'présence pure' of the fountain – 'Je ne veux qu-une seule leçon, c'est la tienne, / fontaine, qui en toi-même retombes ...' – celebrate a terrestrial totality that includes the 'celestial' – '... ce céleste retour vers la vie terrienne' – and the 'open love' of its self-affirmation: [155]

Au lieu de s'évader
ce pays consent à lui-même; ...

. . .

c'est la terre contente de son image
et qui consent à son premier jour

Doubtless if one were to summarise the sentiment of Rilke's work or to find a common denominator in all that vast material of his letter writing, the certainty from which one would start is the attitude of affirmation. To give the evidence for this would be to quote Rilke *passim*. It is more evident than ever in his last years, and it is easy to find scholastically thesis-like statements of absolute affirmation: 'Nur das Nirgends ist böse. / Alles Sein ist gemäß.' In the most intimate letters, like those to Lou Andreas-Salomé, there are rare moments of doubt and depression and one senses how Rilke is at once fascinated and repelled when he speaks of the ageing Michelangelo: '. . . der in einem Sonnet schreibt: was nützt es, noch so viele Puppen gemacht zu haben?', or when he reads in the later Jacobsen: 'Ewig und ohne Veränderung / ist das Leere nur einzig allein. / Alles was ist und war / und was da strebt zum Sein, / wird geweckt im Keimen und geboren, / wechselt, altert, geht in Tod verloren.' But otherwise, and always when he is speaking for himself, he writes in terms of 'bénédiction' and 'consentement'. In a well-known passage from a letter to Princess Marie, describing his chance meeting with a stray dog – one of many similar incidents spoken of by Rilke in terms of mystical encounter – he writes at the end: 'Das kann doch nur auf Erden geschehen, es ist auf alle Fälle gut, hier willig durchgegangen zu sein, wenn auch unsicher, wenn auch schuldig, wenn auch ganz und gar nicht heldenhaft, – man wird am Ende wunderbar auf göttliche Verhältnisse vorbereitet sein.[156]. It is worth noting that Rilke here speaks of going through life 'willingly', lest one understand in too doctrinaire a fashion the fact that Rilke more usually refers in a negative way to exertions of the 'will' as to ambitions of 'understanding'.

6 *Überzähliges Dasein*: the myth of totality

Of the several recurring formulae of affirmation perhaps the most significant is that of 'supernumerous existence' or, as in the Sonnets (2 XXII) 'die herrlichen Überflüsse unseres Daseins,' a theme more particularly dominant in the later years and with which the Ninth Elegy, generally regarded as his 'Botschaft', concludes: 'Überzähliges Dasein / entspringt mir im Herzen.' It is a very firm conclusion, though, being Rilke, it is, as well as being simple and clear, also complex and problematic in all of its terms. The motif of the heart has to do with that Rilkean inwardness that for some critics is his escape into irrationalism and that is, in fact, related to the other motif of 'Überzähligkeit', the prejudice against numbering, naming, knowing, which in turn is part of that concept of 'Dasein' that is the main concern of so much Rilke criticism, whether as something more than human or less than human. 'Zahlenlosigkeit' and similar terms form a word cluster particularly central to the later Rilke, as in 'Sei allem Abschied voran' (2 XIII), the sonnet which he himself said was 'on the whole closest' to him and 'in the end the most valid of all'.[157]

Sei allem Abschied voran, als wäre er hinter
dir, wie der Winter, der eben geht.
Denn unter Wintern ist einer so endlos Winter,
daß, überwinternd, dein Herz überhaupt übersteht.

Sei immer tot in Eurydike —, singender steige,
preisender steige zurück in den reinen Bezug.
Hier, unter Schwindenden, sei, im Reiche der Neige,
sei ein klingendes Glas, das sich im Klang schon zerschlug.

> Sei – und wisse zugleich des Nicht-Seins Bedingung,
> den unendlichen Grund deiner innigen Schwingung,
> daß Du sie völlig vollziehst dieses einzige Mal.
>
> Zu dem gebrauchten sowohl, wie zum dumpfen und stummen
> Vorrat der vollen Natur, den unsäglichen Summen,
> zähle dich jubelnd hinzu und vernichte die Zahl.

It is a mysterious affirmation of existence – a creed that speaks of life's unaccountability can hardly be otherwise – but it has the immediacy as well as mysteriousness of Goethe's 'Stirb und Werde', of which it is Rilke's modern and starker counterpart. But the affirmation is unequivocal none the less, as much so in the Elegies as in the Sonnets. Although 'Bleiben ist nirgends' is the characteristic leitmotif of the Elegies, as 'Wolle die Wandlung' is of the Sonnets, the Ninth Elegy, which is the most exhortatory and messianic, ends with the lines:

> Siehe, ich lebe. Woraus? Weder Kindheit noch Zukunft
> werden weniger. . . . Überzähliges Dasein
> entspringt mir im Herzen.

The sentiment is one expressed by Rilke at every stage. In *Malte* for example: 'Erwartung spielt dabei keine Rolle. Es ist alles da. Alles für immer.' Or in one of the many poems on life's 'superfluity' and the 'divine fullness of nature':

> Denn wer sie innen, wie sie drängt, empfände,
> verhielte sich, erfüllt, in seine Hände . . .
> verhielte sich wie Übermaß und Menge
> und meinte nicht es sei ihm was entgangen . . .
> und staunte nur noch, daß er dies ertrüge:
> die schwankende, gewaltige Genüge.

Writing to his publisher and friend Anton Kippenberg a year before his death, Rilke sends him a poem expressing what he hopes to be his ever more valid, lasting and personal conviction: [158]

> Alles ist Überfluß. Denn genug
> war es schon damals, als uns die Kindheit bestürzte
> mit unendlichem Dasein. Damals schon

war es zu viel. Wie sollten wir jemals Verkürzte
oder Betrogene sein: wir, mit jeglichem Lohn
schon Überbelohnten. . . .

The theme is most evident in the last years and related ever and
again to his own artistic experience, particularly in the miracle
months of 1922. Later in the same year he writes:

> Sie schreiben von dem in jedem Moment schon Erfülltsein,
> schon Überreichsein des inneren Daseins, von einem (wenn man
> nur recht zusieht) alle später möglichen Entbehrungen und
> Verluste schon von vornherein überwiegenden und gleichsam
> widerlegenden – Besitz. – Genau dies habe ich diesen langen
> Winter in der Tiefe meiner Arbeit erfahren, mehr und unwider-
> ruflicher, als ich es bisher wußte: daß das Leben jedem späteren
> Armwerden mit den seine Maße übertrefflichsten Reichtümern
> schon längst zuvorgekommen sei. – Was also bliebe zu fürchten?
> – Nur, daß man dies vergäße!

The theme is sustained, in almost unvarying terms, to the end:

> Von allem, was das Leben mir an Unvorhergesehenem zufügen
> könnte, bleibt die Enttäuschung die entfernteste Möglichkeit;
> manche seiner Gaben, die ich in meiner Arbeit verwirklichen
> konnte, haben mich zu sehr erfüllt und für immer entzückt, als
> daß ich jemals an seiner unwandelbaren Großmut zweifeln
> könnte.[159]

For all that he so often rejects moral judgements, Rilke has
his own values of good and evil, though expressed rather in terms
of 'great' and 'little'. Intensity is the touchstone. What is to be
feared above all is 'diminution'. 'C'est toujours cela qui m'effraie
le plus. . . .' More usually this is expressed in the positive form
of the counsel to regard as 'enlargement' whatever seems to
threaten or oppress: 'Sie wissen ja nicht, ob Ihr Herz nicht mit
ihm gewachsen ist. . . .' 'Nous sommes tous en danger pendant
que nous vivons, mais c'est justement ce danger que nous aimons
puisqu'il élargit nos coeurs en y faisant entrer l'infini.'[160] The
attitude is consistent, although he had rather less faith in the

enrichment of outside involvements than in the more fruitful quarrel with one's self. He had experienced this as a child; he writes to Countess Sizzo '. . . und wie oft später ist es mir bestätigt worden, wenn ich Menschen . . . trüb und aussichtslos verzwistet sah . . . und mir klar wurde, daß ein Streit von gleicher Intensität, in einen Einzelnen geworfen . . . unfehlbar für diesen gedachten Einsamen zu irgendeinem Fortschritt führen müßte.'[161] There is something over-insistent in the many references to a love experience that is so utterly independent of 'Dauer und Verlauf', but invariably he is applying a test of intensity to all aspects of life, including death itself, which he defines as 'die uns durchaus übertreffende Intensität'. Often he distinguishes in this connection between 'Freude' and 'Glück'. 'Freude ist unsäglich mehr als Glück.' Where happiness is concerned with 'Dauer', joy is conceived of as truly creative enrichment, to which categories of retention and loss do not apply. 'Wie schwach muß im Grunde doch das Glück uns beschäftigen, da es uns sofort Zeit läßt, an seine Dauer zu denken und darum besorgt zu sein. . . .' When Rilke is writing in this vein, it seems to carry more conviction where the context is not that of other people's problems and he is speaking rather *pro domo* and on his own attitude to 'things'. 'Längst hab ich mich ja gewöhnt, die gegebenen Dinge nach ihrer Intensität aufzufassen, ohne, soweit das menschlich leistbar ist, um die Dauer besorgt zu sein, – es ist am Ende die beste und diskreteste Art, ihnen alles zuzumuten, – selbst die Dauer.'[162]

Secondary literature on Rilke is notorious for its concern with problems of 'being', and it is worth noting that in one of the many letters of counsel Rilke parenthetically defines 'Sein' as 'die Erfahrung der möglichst vollzähligen inneren Intensität'. This simple definition introduces problems enough, but at least one can be sure they are Rilkean ones, including the familiar one of 'totality'. He is writing in the context of sexual problems and the substance of his advice is: 'Kämpfen Sie arglos . . . Überhaupt sind wir da ganz – vergessen Sie das nicht – auf dem Gebiet der Un-Schuld. . . .' He accuses the religions of having degenerated into moralities, concerned with the peripheral and superficial and making demands on the 'will' – a faculty of which

Rilke speaks in sceptical inverted commas – whereas at the deeper level 'Absage' and 'Erfüllung' are identical: 'Wo das Unendliche g a n z eintritt (sei es als Minus oder Plus), fällt das Vorzeichen weg, das, ach, so menschliche, als der vollendete Weg, der nun gegangen ist, – und was bleibt, ist das Angekommensein, das S e i n!'[163] Rilke himself quickly introduces the more abstract absolutes of being. Yet, like most of his motifs, the totality of being is, as well as complex, also a simple matter of the single-minded tenacity with which Rilke sustains the attitude of so experiencing the moment of life that the sense of deprivation can be called an error, as in the Orphic Sonnet (2 XXI):

> Singe die Gärten, mein Herz, die du nicht kennst; wie in Glas
> eingegossene Gärten, klar, unerreichbar,
> Wasser und Rosen von Isphahan oder Schiras,
> singe sie selig, preise sie, keinem vergleichbar.
>
> Zeige, mein Herz, daß du sie niemals entbehrst.
> Daß sie dich meinen, ihre reifenden Feigen,
> Daß du mit ihren, zwischen den blühenden Zweigen
> wie zum Gesicht gesteigerten Lüften verkehrst.
>
> Meide den Irrtum, daß es Entbehrungen gebe
> für den geschehnen Entschluß, diesen: zu sein!
> Seidener Faden, kamst du hinein ins Gewebe.
>
> Welchem der Bilder du auch im Innern geeint bist
> (sei es selbst ein Moment aus dem Leben der Pein),
> fühl, daß der ganze, der rühmliche Teppich gemeint ist.

The opposition of 'rein' and 'unerreichbar' is related to the general inference in Rilke that a precondition of purity is unattainability, beyond the reach and interference of those faculties of volition and cognition Rilke so often appears to mistrust. But in spite of the complexities in detail, the poem's over-all attitude is clear, although difficult in the sense of making such a total demand. The concept of 'Vollzähligkeit' demands a mental submission to every aspect of life and an act of faith in its innocence, without which there is no fullness of being. The motif is more many-faceted in Rilke's poetry and cannot be isolated in the same way, but where he expounds this belief in his letters it would appear to be in a sense both that imputes impieties and hostilities to human judgements, absolutely and not merely relatively, and that cannot really be reconciled with any of the critical and correcting attitudes, whether in the social or the religious sphere, to which Rilke felt himself so opposed. In the often-quoted letter to Countess Sizzo in which he defines the 'essential meaning' of Elegies and Sonnets as 'die Identität von Furchtbarkeit und Seligkeit', he says: 'Wer nicht der Fürchterlichkeit des Lebens irgendwann, mit einem endgültigen Entschlusse, zustimmt, ja ihr zujubelt, der nimmt die unsäglichen Vollmächte unseres Daseins nie in Besitz. . . .'[164] An affirmation of this nature is the price that man pays for making the wholeness of being truly his own, and to this cherished aspect of his belief, that the apparently hostile is 'ours', Rilke returns again and again. Death is the initiation into the other side of 'our existence', he says in a letter to Countess Schwerin, and adds in parentheses: '. . . was soll ich m e h r betonen: "unseres" oder "Daseins"? Beides ist hier von der schwersten Betonung. . . .'[165] Up to a point these letters are very unequivocal. Perhaps the most drastic formulations of an amoral totality are in a long letter to Countess Dietrichstein, written in 1919 and with some reference to the revolutionary events of the time.[166] The aims of the revolutionaries are dismissed with impatiently rhetorical questions – 'was heißt Freiheit?', 'was heißt Glück?' – and the whole letter is characterised by profound mistrust of man, who has become so fatally opposed to nature. For himself, a precondition of his work has been 'jene Gleichgestimmtheit mit dem Natürlichen', an innocent-looking sentiment that is then, however, the starting-point for his most questionable reflections on 'natural' man. Nature herself has no 'Distanz', does not 'look on', is 'infinitely innocent':

Ihr Bewußtsein besteht in ihrer Vollzähligkeit, weil sie a l l e s enthält, enthält sie auch das Grausame, – der Mensch aber, der nie imstande sein wird, alles zu umfassen, ist nie sicher, wo er das Furchtbare wählt, sagen wir den Mord –, auch schon das

Gegenteil dieses Abgrundes zu enthalten, und so richtet ihn
im selben Augenblick seine Wahl, da sie ihn zu einer Ausnahme
macht, zu einem vereinzelten, vereinseitigten Wesen, welches
ans Ganze nicht mehr angeschlossen ist. Der gute, der rein
entschlossene, der fähige Mensch würde das Böse, das Verhängnis, das Leid, das Unheil, den Tod nicht aus den gegen-
seitigen Verhältnissen ausschließen können, aber wo ihn eines
davon träfe oder er zu Ursache dessen würde, da stünde er nicht
anders da als ein Heimgesuchter in der Natur, oder heimsuchend
wider seinen Willen, wäre er wie der verheerende Bach, der
anschwillt durch irgendwelche herabstürzende Tauwässer, deren
Einmündung in ihm er sich nicht zu verschließen vermag.

One may be repelled by the 'inhumanity', though on closer
analysis of the passage, one's reaction may be rather one of be-
wilderment over those highly ambiguous concepts of choice and
decision that Rilke retains within the context of totalities. The
problem, however, is not so much what Rilke means in these letters
as the relevance of what he here says to his poetry. To deny any
relevance would be very restrictive and seem untrue to Rilke, in
whose spiritual development these ideas are a matter of such
passionate conviction. The danger probably lies in relating in too
direct and too coldly cut-and-dried a manner ideas that must first,
as it were, be humanised and referred back to the concrete poetic
experience before they truly touch on the poetic myth. That it is
still a problematic humanisation is something that Rilke himself
acknowledges. In a letter in which he speakes once more of the
necessity of rejecting names and recognising 'the innocence of injustice', he also confesses to his life-long feeling of uncertainty
as a man among men, and says in one of his most explicit references to the art-experience as his only source of equilibrium:
'. . . wäre nicht überhaupt im so und so oft und seit lange Bildend-
Gewesensein die Erfahrung eines tiefsten, nicht moralischen, ja
kaum menschlichen Gleichgewichtes: ich glaube, ich wüßte mich
nicht leben.'[167]
The relevance to the poetry is closer where the expression of
ideas of totality in the letters is itself more 'poetic'. It is not really

so evasive to say that the more poetic expression, in the many descriptive passages on nature's totality, is truer to the poetry. The attitude is invariable – ' . . . wir kommen dazu, in des Lebens Händen alles gelten zu lassen . . .' – but in so far as any belief is implied when Rilke speaks of totality as 'Gottes Vorsehung', it is a belief in the 'providential' fullness of life that has little to do with any definition of Providence. On the question of Rilke's ultimate belief, perhaps Rilke himself suggests the most valid answer in a letter in which he speaks of the belief behind the *Stundenbuch*, or rather its admixture of unbelief – '. . . Unglauben nicht aus Zweifel, sondern aus Nicht-Wissen und Anfängerschaft' – and in which he sees the relationship to God as a kind of private productivity that defies definition and that certainly has little to do with any argument that might convince others: 'Das Verhältnis zu Gott setzt, so wie ich es einsehe, Produktivität, ja irgend ein, ich möchte sagen wenigstens privates, die anderen nicht überzeugendes Genie der Erfindung voraus, das ich mir so weit getrieben denken kann, daß man auf einmal nicht begreift, was mit dem Namen Gott gemeint ist. . . .'[168]

Rilke is anything but non-committal, however, when it comes to bodies of belief opposed to those attitudes of openness, anonymity, totality. His hostility towards Christianity is underlined by the rudely irritable tone (if only in the always less guarded letters to Princess Marie), so startlingly at variance with his usual manner, when he confesses his 'beinah rabiate Antichristlichkeit':

Die Frucht ist ausgesogen, da heißts einfach, grob gesprochen, die Schalen ausspucken. Und da machen Protestanten und amerikanische Christen immer noch wieder einen Aufguß mit diesem Teegrus, der zwei Jahrtausende gezogen hat, Mohammed war auf alle Fälle das Nächste; wie ein Fluß durch ein Urgebirg bricht er sich durch zu dem e i n e n Gott, mit dem sich so großartig reden läßt jeden Morgen, ohne das Telephon 'Christus', in das fortwährend hineingerufen wird: Holla, wer dort? – und niemand antwortet.[169]

(Quite different is the mythical figure of Christ in Rilke's poetry, in poems like *Christi Höllenfahrt, Emmaus, Auferweckung des*

Lazarus, where on the contrary Christ is a figure of 'openness'.
'... Aber plötzlich brach ein hohes Feuer / in ihm aus, ein solcher
Widerspruch / gegen alle ihre Unterschiede, / ihr Gestorben-,
ihr Lebendigsein. ....') The God of the New Testament would be
too historical and too little anonymous, and of the Christian
Churches Rilke writes to Princess Marie that, by comparison with
the smooth totality of Allah, they 'stick in the throat'.[170] In the
more courteous tones of his letters to Pastor Zimmermann, Rilke
speaks of the other-worldliness of God as that against which he
most reacted ever since his childhood: 'Die Abgetrenntheit, die
endgültig gewordene Jenseitigkeit Gottes erstaunte und beun-
ruhigte mich, seit ich ein Kind war. ...' This is the main burden
of many other letters. If he speaks of God and of Gods, it is 'for
the sake of completeness', he writes in a long letter developing the
idea that, like death, God, too, has been excluded from our lives,
whereas, Rilke underlines: *'man war auch dies'.* This may be an-
thropomorphic, but any such labels are probably misleading. Even
Rilke's 'Diesseitigkeit' is more open than definitive. Speaking once
of the necessity of achieving a 'world-participation', of establish-
ing 'a certain totality of our relationships to the earth', he adds:
'... wäre das nicht der einzige Weg für uns, endlich zu mehr als
nur Irdischem gefaßt zu werden?' In the almost countless 'theological' reflections in Rilke's letters the only development that can
be identified with certainty is towards an ever increasing reticence
and discretion – a reaction, one feels, against the wordiness and
familiarity of the *Geschichten vom lieben Gott* and indeed from
the *Stundenbuch,* whose 'Nachbar Gott' Rilke's philosopher friend,
Kassner, found 'peinlich vor allem anderen', and of which Rilke
himself said later: 'Ich hätte endlos ähnliche Verse weiterdichten
können ... und was dann?' Hence Rilke speaks in his later years
of paying the 'courtoisie' of silence to God, Whose name in all
languages is 'unendlich verschweigbar'.[171] In one of these late
letters he speaks of his earlier 'brotherhood' with God and of his
later 'indescribable discretion'.

... Das Faßliche entgeht, verwandelt sich, statt des Besitzes
erlernt man den Bezug, und es entsteht eine Namenlosigkeit,

die wieder bei Gott beginnen muß, um vollkommen und ohne
Ausrede zu sein . . . die Eigenschaften werden Gott, dem nicht
mehr Sagbaren, abgenommen, fallen zurück an die Schöpfung,
an Liebe und Tod . . . alle Engel entschließen sich, lobsingend
zur Erde!

In suggesting that the sense of possession is replaced by the sense
of relationship, the letter takes up a major poetic theme that for
himself was centred in the art-experience. By definition there is a
certain 'Unfaßlichkeit', but for all that, the letter is not so non-
committal, and commitment to the earth is on the whole the most
consistent note both in the poetry and in the letters of his last
years. Not that it is an entirely new theme in Rilke. In an early
letter to Ellen Key he had written: '. . . das Ziel der ganzen menschlichen Entwicklung ist: Gott und die Erde in demselben
Gedanken denken zu können.' The incomprehensibility, too, is a
theme that goes back to the earlier years, is indeed more insisted
on then, for whereas later he prefers to express the theme of
'open' love in the more positive form of openness to a totality
of earthly existence, in the earlier years the emphasis is more on
the objectlessness itself: 'La prière est un rayonnement de notre
être soudainement incendié, c'est une direction infinie et sans
but. . . .' This definition of prayer is echoed much later in the
long letter to Ilse Blumenthal-Weiß on religion in general and
the religious experience of the Jews in particular. It is one of
Rilke's more involved and speculative reflections, but the kernel is
perhaps when he defines religion as being, not knowledge, not
duty, not any form of 'limitation', but: 'eine Richtung des Herzens' – with the certainly heartfelt corollary: 'Die Forcierung des
Herzens, das und jenes für wahr zu halten, die man gewöhnlich
Glauben nennt, hat keinen Sinn.'[172]
     The train of thought leads back to the centre of Rilke's poetry.
To speak of religion as a 'direction of the heart' may seem very
vague, but in fact Rilke is here using one of the key words of
his world – and one which, far from being too neutral, may seem
all too unequivocally committed in opposition to the rational

and volitional, the moralistic and progressive. The Ninth Elegy,
it will be recalled, concludes with the lines:

Siehe. ich lebe. Woraus? Weder Kindheit noch Zukunft
werden weniger. . . . Überzähliges Dasein
entspringt mir im Herzen.

Again in those many confessional passages just quoted, one notices
the recurring reference to the heart and specifically to the heart
as the infinite place and space that is at once 'ours' and, beyond
any mental and moral limitations, anonymously open to that
totality that comprehends death as well as life – 'Jenseits' as well
as 'Diesseits'. 'Herz' is one, but perhaps the most central of several
terms that suggest the paradox of Rilke's poetry, at once so open
to anonymity and totality and so intensely personal, as the famous
epitaph itself is a paradox of a namelessness that is so Rilkean.
The concept dearest to Rilke to the end, says Mason, and the one
which may be regarded as his gospel: '. . . war aber die, daß
"unser Herz" mehr als Diesseits und Jenseits sei, daß alle beide
auf dieses Herz und darauf allein angewiesen seien. . . .'[173] Viewed
sceptically, the heart motif can be said to be yet another aspect
of Rilke's inner emigration, his flight into inwardness, just as after
his own disgust with his brief excursion into the communal at the
outbreak of war, came what he himself refers to as the pendular
return 'in das verlaßne, namenlose eigne Herz'. The heart is in
tune with totality for it makes no moral distinctions, no mental
reservations, is 'innocently' open to all. Just as Rilke so often
refers to the innocence of life as a whole, so too he refers to the
'Unschuld des Herzens', 'la tendre innocence de notre coeur'.[174]
Where he was writing on the ultimate issues, on his religious convictions, on his attitudes to life and death, he returns again and
again to this theme of the heart's wholeness. Writing to Pastor
Zimmermann he declares his own religious practice:

. . . ja, wenn ich zugleich allgemein und wahr sein wollte, so
müßte ich gestehen, es sei mir doch, zeitlebens, um nichts
anderes zu tun, als in meinem Herzen diejenige Stelle zu
entdecken und zu beleben, die mich in Stand setzen würde,

D

in allen Tempeln der Erde mit der gleichen Berechtigung, mit
dem gleichen Anschluß an das jeweils dort Größeste anzubeten.

Or one thinks of the terms in which, writing to her mother, he
celebrates the life of Wera Knoop, the young girl for whom the
Sonnets to Orpheus were a memorial:

> . . . und auf der anderen Seite dieses einige Einssein ihres, allem
> erschlossenen Herzens m i t dieser Einheit der seienden und
> währenden Welt, diese Zusage ans Leben, dieses freudige, dieses
> gerührte, dieses bis ins Letzte fähige Hineingehören ins Hiesige –
> ach, ins Hiesige nur?! Nein, (was sie nicht wissen konnte in
> diesen ersten Angriffen des Abbruchs und Abschieds!) – ins
> G a n z e, in ein viel mehr als Hiesiges. Oh, wie, wie liebte
> sie, wie reichte sie mit den Antennen ihres Herzens über alles
> hier Erfaßliche und Umfängliche hinaus. . . .'

Or finally one may refer again to the letter to Countess Sizzo in
1923, one of the longest of his many long letters of condolence, in
which he speaks of the 'sphere and globe of being', of that totality
in which death itself is understood without negation, this being
the burden of all religious initiation mysteries. Once more he
accuses present-day religions of not accepting death, of approaching it with palliatives, and the letter is uncompromising in rejecting any kind of consolation that would conceal the terrors of
death and the terrible aspect of life. Yet he is also suggesting that
death is hostile only because a mentality of 'Rechnen und Aus-
wählen' has excluded it, and the implication throughout is that
the heart can heal this breach, is indeed an eternal heaven of inwardness. 'Ach, wie wenig v e r g i ß t es, das Herz,' he writes,
and again: '. . . w o schließlich kann er [der Tod] eins, das wir
unsäglich im Herzen getragen haben, anders hin verdrängen, als
in eben dieses Herz, wo wäre die "Idee" dieses geliebten Wesens, ja
seine unaufhörliche Wirkung (: denn w i e könnte d i e aufhören, die
doch schon, da es mit uns lebte, von seiner greifbaren Gegenwart
mehr und mehr unabhängig war) . . . wo wäre diese immer schon
geheime Wirkung gesicherter, als in uns?' However sceptical one
may be about the attitude to 'greifbare Gegenwart', and conscious

of the psychological factors behind it, the passionate intensity
is impressive with which Rilke develops this contradiction-cancel-
ling mythical image of the heart, the 'Grand-Maître des absences':
'. . . das Schlafende und das Wache, das Lichte und das Dunkle,
die Stimme und das Schweigen . . . la présence et l'absence. Alle
die scheinbaren Gegenteile, die irgendwo, in einem Punkt zusam-
menkommen, die an einer Stelle die Hymne ihrer Hochzeit singen
– und diese Stelle ist – vor der Hand – unser Herz!'[175]

7 *Cet ineffable accord*: Rilke's epitaph

This kind of emphasis inevitably makes Rilke's poetry singularly difficult to analyse, if also, even for readers with many reservations, a peculiarly intense experience – but then Rilke himself would be less concerned with, and less convinced by, the analysis than the experience. It is not untypical that 'Verstehen' should be in quotation marks when he writes of the Sonnets that they should rather be understood 'mittels der Eingebung des Gleichgerichteten, als mit dem, was man "Verstehen" nennt. . . .'[176] Only a superficial reading of Rilke would confuse his inwardness with mere sentimentality or an unprofessional vagueness. It is rather in its apparent opposition to consciousness that the 'Herz-Werk' of Rilke's poetry is questionable. But one must be sure that one understands the motif. Apart from the obvious fact that Rilke is a so very self-conscious poet and that the ideal attitude, allegedly so natural, is also very much a 'work' and something over which Rilke agonised and on which he reflected in so many scores of letters, it seems important to relate it to the art-experience from which it is derived. He is suggesting an ideal heart-attitude that somehow contrasts with ordinary consciousness and that is an artistic stage beyond even the intense 'seeing' of the artist's 'Werk des Gesichts'. 'Da geht das Herz und geht und sieht nicht her,' he writes in the fourth of the *Capreser Improvisationen*, the poem *Nun schließe deine Augen*:

Schließ, schließ fest die Augen. War es dies?

Du weißt es nicht. Du kannst es schon nicht mehr
von Deinem Herzen trennen.

Himmel im Innern läßt sich schwer
erkennen;
da geht das Herz und geht und sieht nicht her.

Und doch Du weißt: wir können also so
am Abend zugehn wie die Anemonen,
die Tiefe eines Tages in sich schließend,
und, etwas größer, morgens wieder aufgehn.
Und das zu tun ist uns nicht nur erlaubt,
das ist es, was wir s o l l e n : z u g e h n   l e r n e n
ü b e r   U n e n d l i c h e m.

Clearly he claims a 'knowing' derived from the artistic experience,
and the 'not-knowing' itself is in the first place a paradoxical
aspect and precondition of that experience:[177]

Wenn irgendwo ein Kindgewesensein
tief in mir aufsteigt, das ich noch nicht kenne,
vielleicht das reinste Kindsein meiner Kindheit:
ich wills nicht wissen. Einen Engel will
ich daraus bilden ohne hinzusehn. . . .

That the artist creates 'without looking' is one element in a whole
cluster of motifs in Rilke, in whose work negatives are so often
positive in the context of the open attitude. The many variations
of objectlessness, for example, prayer that is 'sans but' or art that,
like music, is 'von jeglichem Wozu befreit'. Or again the frequent
appositions of 'Nirgendshin' and 'Seligkeit'. The passage in the
Seventh Elegy: 'wie überholtet ihr oft den Geliebten, atmend, /
atmend nach seligem Lauf, auf nichts zu, ins Freie' recalls the
description in *Die Treppe der Orangerie*: 'so steigt, allein zwischen den Balustraden, / die sich verneigen schon seit Anbeginn, /
die Treppe: langsam und von Gottes Gnaden / und auf den Himmel zu und nirgends hin. . . .' Or the description of the carillon
in a letter to Frau Wunderly-Volkart: 'Die Glockenspiele spielen
immerzu . . . ein Auf und Ab, kleine Leitern für das Herz, hinauf
und hinunter, nirgends hin, aber an seeliger Stelle.'[178] Similarly,
'blindness' is associated with that 'Lächeln', which in Rilke is an
expression of basic affirmation: '. . . denn das Lächeln ist nichts,

als das consentement des Geistes, in uns zu sein.' At the
end of *Das Karusell*, for example: '. . . Und manchesmal ein
Lächeln, hergewendet / ein seliges, das blendet und verschwendet
/ an dieses atemlose blinde Spiel. . . .'[179] And above all in the
flowery baroque imagery in the Fifth Elegy of the 'subrisio salta-
toris', preserved in the apothecary's urn with its 'florally soaring
inscription':

> Und dennoch, blindlings,
> das Lächeln . . .
> Engel! o nimms, pflücks, das kleinblütige Heilkraut.
> Schaff eine Vase, verwahrs! Stells unter jene, uns n o c h nicht
> offenen Freuden; in lieblicher Urne
> rühms mit blumiger schwungiger Aufschrift:
>   'Subrisio Saltat'.

The motif of the artist, who 'does not look' or 'looks away' is
obviously related to the theme referred to earlier of the 'pure
danger' that, for those who are totally open to life and do not
'distinguish', becomes protection:

> Hier sei uns Alles Heimat: auch die Not.
> wer wagt, was uns geschieht, zu unterscheiden?
> Vielleicht macht uns das Leiden leidend leiden;
> und wenn wir wegschaun, schützt uns, was uns droht.

Although it is couched in positive terms, there is undoubtedly,
hidden in all this imagery of inwardness, a profound mistrust of
the doings of men, of the critical mind and the interfering will.
Fortunately life ultimately eludes their grasp: 'Gekonnt hats
keiner; denn das Leben währt / weils keiner konnte. . . . Weils
keiner meistert, bleibt das Leben rein. . . .'[180] It would be de-
humanising the poetry not to allow any link between this theme
and, at the level of opinion and prejudices, the general trend of
Rilke's attitude in the more day-to-day comments of his letters.
From the beginning he felt himself out of sympathy with what he
termed in a letter to Stefan Zweig this 'im Kritischen allzu geüb-
ten Zeit'. His attitude to the 'will' remained hostile, as one sees
from the comment in one of the late letters:

Wievieles, was sonst mit dem Gang der normalen Strömungen einem zutrieb, muß man jetzt w o l l e n, um es zu erreichen – , und darüber wird die Welt indiskret und verkrampft; denn das Beste, uns natürlich Zukommende, entstellt sich schon allein dadurch, daß es in die ungeduldigen Bereiche des Willens einbezogen wird. . . .'

Benvenuta reports his comment on Ibsen: . . .

> aber das Größeste hatte er nicht: sein Herz reichte nicht aus, es war nicht willig genug hinzunehmen, er holte sich Rat bei der kältesten Vernunft – und so entstand Tendenz, Meinung und das verbissenste Verfechten dieser 'Meinung'. . . .

Even of Werfel, who, one would have thought, was hardly lacking in 'heart', he says in a letter to Princess Marie that he was 'trop intelligent peut-être pour sa poésie', with a too reflective spirit and an 'esprit juif' at that.[181] Although one must not read too much into the mood of a moment, sweeping rejections like this are typical enough:

> . . . Es ist ja immer wieder das 'Ganze', worum sichs da handelt, dieses Ganze aber, wenn wirs auch innerlich manchmal zusammenfassen in einem Elan des Glücks oder des reinen Willens, in der Wirklichkeit ists unterbrochen durch alle die Irrtümer, Fehler, Unzulänglichkeiten, durch das Bösartige von Mensch zu Mensch, durch das Rastlose und Trübe – , ja beinah durch alles, was uns täglich angeht.

There is little in the way of human activity that escapes mistrust here – and in the orphic mythology itself such mistrust of humanity and its 'will to know' is an element at least:

> Immer wieder von uns aufgerissen,
> ist der Gott die Stelle, welche heilt!
> Wir sind Scharfe, denn wir wollen wissen,
> aber er ist heiter und verteilt. . . .

In another of the conversations reported by Benvenuta, in which again he speaks of the harmony of 'heart' and nature, the closing remark, while casting doubt on knowledge, also suggests his life-long struggle to find for himself and to express in his poetry a 'world-view' as opposed to a merely human perspective: ' "... aber schließlich: was wissen wir!" schloß er seufzend, "reicht denn nicht im Grunde alles über uns hinaus, über unser Innigstes und Geringstes, hat denn nicht alles um uns in der Welt Gesetz und Geltung auch o h n e uns?" '[182]. Again and again he celebrates whatever in nature can seem to dissolve distinctions in a 'world-participation', like the bird-song of which he speaks in the letter to Lou Andreas-Salomé, that can momentarily initiate us into this 'Weltinnenraum'. He regarded himself above all as a poet of 'things'. 'Meine Welt beginnt bei den D i n g e n,' he writes, and again: 'Ich habe das eigentümliche Glück, durch die D i n g e zu leben. . . .' If there is an element of escape from the claims and problems of reflective life when he so often cele-brates in things 'wie sie so gar keine Anhänglichkeit haben, so ganz unsentimental sind', it is an aspect of the search for 'being' – and, before one dismisses the term as either an unhelpful or an inhuman one, one should allow for its setting in the context of Rilke's understanding of art, where, though there may be a similar prejudice against reflection and explanation, the appeal to mystery will not strike one in the same doctrinaire way as anti-rational or inhuman. Writing of her paintings to Sophy Giauque he says: 'De tels secrets ne sont pas là pour être exprimés et expliqués, ils sont secrets de la façon la plus franche, comme on est chien et pomme. . . .'[183] Even the experience of death is set in the context of – or in a context analogous to that of – nature's 'simply being'. In a letter of condolence to Freiin Schenk he apologises for the re-moteness and apparent coldness of his answer:

> . . . Aber Sie hatten gefragt, und ich mußte so weit steigen, um Ihnen meine Antwort in den Zusammenhängen zu zeigen, in denen allein sie nicht trostlos aussieht, sondern (das fühlen Sie doch) – gut, oder einfach s e i e n d über alles Urteil hinaus, wie die Natur seiend ist, die uns nicht verstehen will und uns doch hält und uns hilft.

The sphere of being 'über alles Urteil hinaus' may seem an un-
attainable or inhuman refuge, but Rilke rings the changes on the
theme of human 'Wirrnis':

Natur ist glücklich. Doch in uns begegnen
sich zuviel Kräfte, die sich wirr bestreiten:
wer hat ein Frühjahr innen zu bereiten?
Wer weiß zu scheinen? Wer vermag zu regnen? . . .

Moreover, one of the earliest, strongest and most sustained themes
is that of the earth-like existence that he speaks of in a letter
to his wife: '. . . und wir haben im Grunde nur d a z u s e i n,
aber schlicht, aber inständig, wie die Erde da ist, den Jahreszeiten zustimmend, hell und dunkel und ganz im Raum, nicht
verlangend in anderem aufzuruhen als in dem Netz von Einflüssen
und Kräften, in dem die Sterne sich sicher fühlen.' It may be fair
to say that Rilke and his poetry, which in any case is not, in any
normal sense of the term, nature poetry, are anything but
'schlicht', but then when Rilke is speaking of natural 'being' it
is not as the exclusion of consciousness but as the inclusion of
'totality'. His very manner of speaking of it is almost wilfully
human, and in that letter in which he speaks of man's exclusion
of God and death, a suppression of which nature knows nothing,
it is not preciosity, still less sentimentality, but an attempt to
maintain the mythology of total commitment – which may indeed
be superhuman and in that sense inhuman – when he goes on:
'. . . und über all um uns ist der Tod noch zu Haus und aus den
Ritzen der Dinge sieht er uns zu, und ein rostiger Nagel, der
irgendwo aus einer Planke steht, tut Tag und Nacht nichts, als sich
freuen über ihn.'[184]
In the orphic sonnet 'Giebt es wirklich die Zeit, die zerstörende?'
(2 XXVII), the infinity of the heart is invoked again in fulfilment
of the infinite promise of childhood:

. . .

Sind wir wirklich so ängstlich Zerbrechliche,
wie das Schicksal uns wahr machen will?

Ist die Kindheit, die tiefe, versprechliche,
in den Wurzeln – später – still?

Ach, das Gespenst des Vergänglichen,
durch den arglos Empfänglichen
geht es, als wär es ein Rauch.

. . .

Like so much else in Rilke, the motif of time, too, has a double
aspect, of belittlement and loss or of what one might call 'time-
fulness'. Hence, though one may, up to a point speak of the time
imagery of the Elegies being answered by the space imagery of the
Sonnets, the contrast needs to be qualified. Beda Allemann
stresses that in the later Rilke 'timelessness' is never the answer,
that 'zeitlos' is as much a negative as 'todlos' and that the space
imagery includes time, just as concepts of motion are essential
to Rilke's 'figure' imagery. In the last years especially this complex of motifs issues in the sense of the 'fullness of time'. With
whatever degree of conviction this is communicated – and Rilke
himself makes it clear that against the 'simple' attitude of what
he likes to call 'Arglosigkeit' is ranged the whole complex of
those attitudes associated with 'Verstand' and 'Kritik', 'Neugier'
and 'Tendenz', 'naming' and 'numbering', – Rilke would seem to
claim that such a stage of intensity and openness is humanly
possible and that for the totally receptive totality is recreated. So
he speaks of the 'divine' comfort within human experience itself
in a letter to Princess Marie:

. . . sondern es müßte nur unser Auge eine Spur schauender,
unser Ohrempfangender sein, der Geschmack einer Frucht
müßte uns vollständiger eingehen, wir müßten mehr Geruch
aushalten, und im Berühren und Angerührtsein geistesgegen-
wärtiger und weniger vergeßlich sein – : um sofort aus unseren
nächsten Erfahrungen Tröstungen aufzunehmen, die überzeugender, wahrer wären als alles Leid, das uns je erschüttern
kann.[185]

For this 'Offenheit' and 'Arglosigkeit', the most frequent metaphor in his poetry is that of 'flowering'. 'Ach wers verstünde zu

blühn: dem wär das Herz über alle / schwachen Gefahren hinaus
und in der großen getrost.' One of his late dedicatory poems
begins:

> Weiß die Natur noch den Ruck,
> da sich ein Teil der Geschöpfe
> abriß vom stätigen Stand?
> Blumen, geduldig genug,
> hoben nur horchend die Köpfe,
> blieben im Boden gebannt . . .

and the poem ends with the italicised line:

> uns sei Blume – sein groß.

The anemone in particular is the model of openness, as in the
fourth of the *Capreser Improvisation*, quoted above, and particularly in the orphic sonnet (2 V) with its celebration of that so
very Rilkean measure of energy and power, the muscle of the
flower:

> Blumenmuskel, der der Anemone
> Wiesenmorgen nach und nach erschließt,
> bis in ihren Schooß das polyphone
> Licht der lauten Himmel sich ergießt,
>
> in den stillen Blütenstern gespannter
> Muskel des unendlichen Empfangs,
> manchmal s o von Fülle übermannter,
> daß der Ruhewink des Untergangs
>
> kaum vermag die weitzurückgeschnellten
> Blätterränder dir zurückzugeben:
> du, Entschluß und Kraft von w i e viel Welten!
>
> Wir, Gewaltsamen, wir währen länger.
> Aber w a n n, in welchem aller Leben,
> sind wir endlich offen und Empfänger?

In a letter to Lou Andreas-Salomé Rilke writes: 'Ich bin wie
die kleine Anemone, die ich einmal in Rom im Garten gesehen
habe, sie war tagsüber so weit aufgegangen, daß sie sich zur

Nacht nicht mehr schließen konnte. . . .'[186] In the particular context the reference is mainly to aspects of 'exposure' and 'dissipation' in the attitude of openness, but the over-all reference is to that receptivity, that sense of 'astonishment' that he again and again claims as the fundamental impulse of his artistic creativity: '. . . Da doch letzten Grundes meine Produktivität aus der unmittelbaren Bewunderung des Lebens, aus dem täglichen unerschöpflichen Staunen vor ihm hervorgeht. . . .' This attitude is the precondition of true creativity and insight: '. . . denn man leistets mit dem Staunen vor allem, je mehr man davon aufbringt, desto näher reicht man hier an die Dinge heran. . . .' It goes without saying that it is a very self-reflective and deflected sense of 'seeing' and 'being' in the case of Rilke. One can fully accept it, not only as a heartfelt wish, but as an implied claim, when Rilke writes to Princess Marie how much he wishes for himself '. . . so viel Fassung in mein Herz, solchen Gegenständen gegenüber dazusein, still, aufmerksam, als ein Seiendes, Schauendes, Um-sich-nicht-Besorgtes . . .', while at the same time admitting that few poets, or bodies of poetry, are so 'um-sich-besorgt'. Similarly one can accept as genuine the sentiments of the Kappus letters, the aversion to names and to approaching life: 'mit Vorwürfen (das heißt: moralisch)', the counsel to let things 'simply happen', while recognising the irony in the fact that it should be Rilke writing: 'Beobachten Sie sich nicht zu sehr. . . .' But then in his concern with himself, Rilke is the most penetrating observer of his own paradoxes. Rather than assume in too abstract and absolute a sense that the ideal of 'thing' or 'plant' is inhuman, one should accept, for example, the more tentative and qualified way in which Rilke indicates his attitude in a letter to Frau Wunderly-Volkart: '. . . ein gewisser eigensinniger e f f o r t des Menschlichen ist mir fremd geworden, – die Pflanze, das Ding – sie schämen sich auch nicht, wenn sie es gut und richtig haben, sie gedeihen einfach und sind, was zu sein ihnen gegeben ist, mit vollkommener Freude.'[187]

One is left with that complexity of uncertainties and certainties for which the last word is the famous epitaph, which Rilke dictated in his will the year before his death:

Rose, oh reiner Widerspruch, Lust
Niemandes Schlaf zu sein unter soviel
Lidern.

Inevitably a great deal of speculation has centred around this
gnomic little poem, and for some it as surely refers to the dis-
appearance of the person, as to others its message is immortality.
Exquisite though it is, it probably lends itself all too easily to an
over-romanticised reading of Rilke, particularly with so much
supporting material to hand, from the very precious gesture recorded in the early Worpsweder diary – 'Ich erfand mir eine neue
Zärtlichkeit: eine Rose leise auf das geschlossene Auge zu legen,
bis sie mit ihrer Kühle kaum mehr fühlbar ist und nur die Sanft-
mut ihres Blattes noch über dem Lid ruht, wie [ein Stück] Schlaf
vor Sonnenaufgang'[188] – to that true-incident-become-legend from
the end of his life: how, gathering a bouquet in his rose garden
at Muzot for his Egyptian friend, Madame Eloui Bey, he cut his
hand on a thorn, the resulting infection leading to the discovery
of his leukemia.

It would almost certainly be mistaken to approach the epitaph
as if a single meaning could be traced from clues of detail elsewhere in his work, for example by cross-reference to the French
prose-poem, *Cimetière*, apparently written shortly before. There
the emphasis is more clearly on the reluctance of the flowers to
be 'ours' or anything but themselves, though the theme is couched
throughout in question form: '. . . Comment ne pas être n o s
fleurs? Est-ce de tous ses pétales que la rose s'éloigne de nous?
Veut-elle être rose-seule, rien-que-rose? Sommeil de personne sous
tant de paupières?'[189] In Rilke's poetry the rose, as flower of
flowers, 'fleur de toutes nos fleurs', is clearly intended as the
culminating symbol for its celebration of existence, the most
fitting memorial for the poet as for Orpheus (1 V):

Errichtet keinen Denkstein. Laßt die Rose
nur jedes Jahr zu seinen Gunsten blühn.
Denn Orpheus ists. Seine Metamorphose
in dem und dem. Wir sollen uns nicht mühn

um andre Namen. Ein für alle Male
ists Orpheus, wenn es singt. Er kommt und geht.
Ists nicht schon viel, wenn er die Rosenschale
um ein paar Tage manchmal übersteht?

O wie er schwinden muß, daß ihrs begrifft!
Und wenn ihm selbst auch bangte, daß er schwände.
Indem sein Wort das Hiersein übertrifft,

ist er schon dort, wohin ihrs nicht begleitet.
Der Leier Gitter zwängt ihm nicht die Hände.
Und er gehorcht, indem er überschreitet.

The rose symbolises the challenge of existence itself, the 'work
of being'. 'Car ce n'est pas travailler que d'être / une rose, dirait-
on.' It is the supreme symbol of 'présence pure', the 'rose complète', 'rose toute la vie', the 'chose par excellence complète /
qui se contient infinement'. Yet as in that 'most valid' orphic
sonnet it is a being that accepts its 'accord' with non-being: [190]

Ton innombrable état te fait-il connaître
dans un mélange où tout se confond,
cet ineffable accord du néant et de l'être
que nous ignorons?

Similarly it is paradoxical in its symbolism of narcissistic self-
containment. Again and again the rose poems celebrate the 'thème
du Narcisse'. 'C'est ton intérieur qui sans cesse / se caresse,
dirait-on . . .'; 'c'est qu-en toi-même, en dedans, / pétale contre
pétale, tu te reposes . . .'; 'C'est toi qui prépares en toi / plus
que toi, ton ultime essence. . . .' Yet as in the earlier poem, *Die
Rosenschale*, it is a flower of 'lauter Augenlider' that is at once
'sheer inwardness', 'lauter Inneres', and an 'outermost' or 'utter-
most' of being, '. . . das unser sein mag: Äußerstes auch uns'.[191]
The poem ends with the paradox of open self-containment in the
transformation into inwardness:

Und sind nicht alle so, nur sich enthaltend,
wenn Sich-enthalten heißt: die Welt da draußen

und Wind und Regen und Geduld des Frühlings
und Schuld und Unruh und vermummtes Schicksal
und Dunkelheit der abendlichen Erde
bis auf der Wolken Wandel, Flucht und Anflug
bis auf den vagen Einfluß ferner Sterne
in eine Hand voll Innres zu verwandeln.

Nun liegt es sorglos in den offnen Rosen.

It may seem facile to appeal to paradox, but then mysteries of
the One and the Many are hardly less mysterious in the more
established orthodoxies. More justifiable is the reaction against
Rilke's inwardness – and whatever about being the culmination of
the German death-wish, Rilke's poetry does seem to be the
culmination of German inwardness. Even the Duino Elegies, in
spite of their wider range, are an extraordinarily self-centred work,
however obvious the implication that the poetic experience is paradigmatic and more than personal. But the inwardness, although
so unpromising if one is looking in the first place for the historical
and communicable, is Rilke's form of concern for life and saves
his poetry from the colder aesthetics of the self-concern of the
work of art 'an sich'. In one sense, of course, Rilke is an aesthete,
and very much so in the practical matters of sheltered protection
and the private life he cultivated so intensely and publicised so
widely. One can read with some irreverence what one comes to
regard, unjustly but understandably, as his correspondence with
countless countesses. One reads with mixed feelings his own references to that vast output, as when he complains to Merline of the
number of letters (on this particular occasion: one hundred and
fifteen) he has to write to 'jeunes filles terriblement abandon-
nées' and 'jeunes mariées effrayées de ce que leur est arrivé'.[192]
Even at the more theoretical level, if one feels that he is a
poor subject for 'Kommunikationswissenschaft', Rilke himself
has, again and again, made statements on art that would seem to
confirm the worst suspicions of his more hostile critics. The public
has long ago forgotten, he complains in one of his later letters,
that the work of art is not an object offered to it 'sondern ein in
ein imaginäres Dasein und Dauer rein hineingestellter, und daß

sein Raum, eben dieser Raum seines Dauerns, nur scheinbar identisch ist mit dem Raume der öffentlichen Bewegungen und Umsätze'. 'Von "Wirkung" ist da nirgends die Rede . . . ,' as he says in another letter. He is very determined to distinguish between the colloquial word and the word of poetry, 'unbrauchbar für den bloßen Umgang', and speaks of the strange obligation of the poet: '. . . sein Wort von den Worten des bloßen Umgangs und der Verständigung gründlich, wesentlich zu unterscheiden. . . '. Similarly he writes to his publisher that the language of his work is not in the first instance, 'Deutsch', but rather 'Gedicht'.[193] While much of this, as in the letter to Kippenberg, which is really a plea for protection, is prompted by his just assessment of his own strength and weaknesses, and by his embarrassment, as he says, in the face of any 'Zu-Worte-Kommen' and 'Vor-den-Vorhang-Treten', it does seem to associate his art with the kind of word-cult and cult of the unhistorical and lonely artefact one associates with Benn's 'Artistik'. Yet overall it is the fundamental difference that strikes one most, for ultimately what matters is the 'inner event'.

> Auch das Hervorbringen, selbst das produktivste, dient ja nur der Schaffung einer gewissen inneren Konstanten, und Kunst ist vielleicht nur deshalb so viel, weil einzelne ihrer reinsten Bildungen eine Gewähr geben für die Erreichung einer zuverlässigen inneren Einstellung. . . .

What the artist intends, in Rilke's formulation, is only 'also' the work of art, for he means even more the invisible and inward achievement of a 'wholer' state of being:

> Denn so sehr der Künstler in einem auch das Werk meint, seine Verwirklichung, sein Dasein und Dableiben über uns hinaus –, ganz gerecht wird man erst, wenn man einsieht, daß auch diese dringendste Realisierung einer höheren Sichtbarkeit, von einem unendlich äußersten Ausblick aus, nur als Mittel erscheint, ein wiederum Unsichtbares, ganz und gar Inneres und vielleicht Unscheinbares –, einen heileren Zustand in der Mitte des eigenen Wesens zu gewinnen.'[194]

It would be misleading, therefore, to say merely of the epitaph that it points away from the poet to his memorial in the 'immortality' of art. Certainly the person of the poet seems to recede, and the epitaph reminds one of a phrase from a letter to a young reader, who had written to him in his last years, in which he does point away from himself to the more valid forms of his work, for, as for himself: 'Wer weiß, wer ich bin? ich wandle und wandle mich.'[195] It is almost like a paraphrase, in part at least, of the epitaph, for the epitaph is, in part, an openly inconclusive myth of the transformations of existence. But then the epitaph is so appropriate to Rilke precisely because, side by side with the certainties of affirmative attitude are its uncertainties of presence and absence, the ambiguities of anonymity – and it is a final conceit not untypical of Rilke to have the name (reiner) and songs (Lider) of the poet hidden in this anonymity. If it is paradoxical that Rilke should speak so longingly of his wish to look away, to be 'um-sich-nicht-besorgt', it is no less ironic that secondary literature on Rilke's 'anonyme Kunst' should be so very concerned with biography and background, to the point that some may feel it is like discussing a painter's opinions to the neglect of painterly qualities. Yet there is probably some inevitability about a response so universal. Michael Hamburger suggests that 'inestimable harm has been done to Rilke's work by the posthumous publication of his letters and private documents'.[196] Undoubtedly that material points up the negative elements that went to the making of his poetry and the extent to which his art was an escape. There was one period in his later life when 'reality' almost broke through the barriers and, as he said, what he had so carefully transfigured in his art threatened to reappear in all its original 'senselessness'. His fears are painfully evident, especially as unburdened in the letters to Marie von Thurn und Taxis. 'Ich fürchte nichts mehr, als mit irgend welchen Behörden in Konflikt zu gerathen', he writes to the Princess, and his feelings of paralysis during those war years are expressed to her in terms of the wretched realities of his boyhood: 'Es geht mir jetzt damit, wie es mir als Knabe in der Turnstunde ging – ich nehme einen rasenden Anlauf – , aber ich kann nicht springen.' If he makes no small claim for his art,

outside of it he renounces any claim whatsoever. 'Daß ich
wünsche, Gott möchte mich, solang als möglich, an meiner
Arbeit lassen . . . das wird mir keiner verdenken, der weiß,
wie ich zu dieser Arbeit steh, und begreift, daß ich *in* ihr
eine Macht und Herrlichkeit bin und außer ihr nicht einmal
ein Kräftchen.'[197] He may have spoken more openly to the Princess
than to others, but throughout his letters, and for all that in so
many hundreds of them he acts as counsellor and pronounces on
life and death, he is at pains to separate poetic insight from any
mundane competence: 'Das, was in einem Gedicht oder sonst
einem Kunstwerk an Gelingen und Einsicht glücklich zusammen-
kommt, ist ja nicht zugleich Bewältigung und Können des täglichen Lebens. . . .' For a poet the whole affliction and blessedness
of his life must be within his work: '. . . und das äußere Leben
muß davon geprägt sein, daß man sich weigert, sie beide anderswo
durchzumachen.' Taken literally, Rilke's pronouncements on
an art that is 'alleinseligmachend' are stubbornly absolutist –
'. . . denn in der Kunst ist wirklich Raum für alle Gegensätzlichkeiten der inneren Verhältnisse, nur in ihr. . . .'[198] Certainly he
claims a wide analogous significance for his mythology of art,
as expressed not only in the myths of Angel and Orpheus, but in
so many other variations on the same theme, but it seems that he
cannot express often enough, or strongly enough, the singularity
of his commitment: 'Immer mehr habe ich in meiner Arbeit alle
Zustimmung und allen Widerspruch, alle Rettung und alle Gefahr,
die es im Himmel und auf Erden geben kann. Ich beruhe unendlich
restlos in ihr: auf Tod und Leben.' It may be impossible to avoid
the conclusion that this narrows the base of Rilke's poetry. One
can only suggest that it has its own form of breadth in the wider
life-long context. For Rilke himself, in any case, it seems certain
that his primary aim was that artistic 'being' to which he refers
in an early letter, when he says: '. . . nur die ganz Großen *sind*
Künstler in jenem strengen, aber einzig wahren Sinn, daß die
Kunst eine Art zu leben für sie geworden ist. . . .'[199]

　　If Rilke so much stresses his 'insignificance' outside of his
work, the conclusion does not follow that those letters and private
documents are irrelevant to the poetry. At least it did not follow

for Rilke himself, who regarded them as part of what he had to
'give', 'Teil der Ergiebigkeit meiner Natur', as he said in his will,
in which he more-than-authorised their publication. This does not,
of itself, answer the objection that there is something negative
about referring the orphic myth of Rilke's poetry back to the
attitudes and reactions of his private life, as it were reversing the
process of his own 'Umschlag' into the positives of his art. It is to
some extent a deflating and even demythologising exercise, but it
is also a way of taking the myth seriously and humanising it. Some
will prefer a more work-immanent approach and, in fact, while it
is true that the spate of publications continues, these have taken a
different direction and the more typical works of recent years have
been highly technical studies on linguistic and rhetorical issues –
sometimes so uncompromisingly academic, they bring to mind
Rilke's remark that he never read what was written on his work
in journals 'oder gar in schon nach "Wissenschaft" schmeckenden
Büchern'.[200] It is a long time since books on Rilke the seer and
God-seeker were in vogue. Yet one feels that it is still in the context
of a life-story of poetry lived with such extraordinary concentration and intensity that Rilke has most to offer. Even apart from
the fact that it serves to reveal the drama of the Elegies, one
would not wish to miss for its own sake the documentation of so
intense an experience of existence, from the special pleading of
the early letters and the climactic experiences of Duino and
Muzot to the pathos of the last letters, like the letter to Jules
Supervielle in which, a week before his death, he refers for the
last time to the 'dictionary' of the earth that gave him words for
life: [201]

Mon cher cher Supervielle,
gravement malade, douloureusement, misérablement, humble-
ment malade, je me retrouve un instant dans la douce conscience
d'avoir pu être rejoint, même là, sur ce plan insituable et si peu
humain, par votre envoi et par toutes les influences qu'il
m'apporte.
　　Je pense à vous, poète, ami, et faisant cela je pense encore
le monde, pauvre débris d'un vase qui se souvient d'être de la

terre. (Mais cet abus de nos sens et de leur 'dictionnaire' par la douleur qui le feuillette!)

The opinion was quoted at the outset that Rilke's philosophy has, by now, been 'debunked'. Perhaps there never was a philosophy in the first place, but there surely was an existential confrontation of quite extraordinary intensity. In spite of his extreme self-centredness, or perhaps because of the total dedication with which he lived the life of poetry, Rilke is an experience as few other poets are. It is not a question of seeing his poetry in some remote context beyond any considerations of truth or falsity. On the contrary, his poetry pre-eminently provokes a response in terms of the rightness or wrongness of this mythology of life. J. B. Leishman wrote a generation ago in his introduction to his translation of the Sonnets: 'In this age of shifting foundations and looming catastrophes, when quacks are bawling their nostrums from every stall, it is worthwhile to consider very seriously this man who, though he might sometimes be gravely mistaken, spent a lifetime of such passionate insight and imagination *de novissimis*, concerning the last things; who reached frontiers and cross-roads that we too may be approaching and where we too will be compelled to pause and to decide. . . .' True, this is a very eschatological kind of approach to poetry. Mason, in his acid way, derived much pleasure from listing his fellow-critics and the certainties which they believed they had got from Rilke, about existence and eternity, God and the good life, all of which Rilke could not give, because he did not have it, nor, in Mason's view, want to have it, himself.[202] But then Mason was not in a position to accuse others of being over-concerned with the person and opinions of Rilke at the expense of purely poetic considerations. Sceptics and believers seem equally to have found rewarding the more personal encounter with Rilke. One would be hard put to it to defend this kind of approach to poetry as a general principle. But perhaps one should not worry too much about the principle if, in the particular case of Rilke, it still proves fruitful in practice.

References

1 Heinrich Meyer, *Was bleibt: Bemerkungen über Literatur und Leben, Schein und Wirklichkeit* (Stuttgart: 1966).
2 Michael Hamburger, *The Truth of Poetry* (Pelican Books, 1972) p. 111.
3 *Straßentheater*, ed. Agnes Hüfner (Suhrkamp, 1970) pp. 88 ff.
4 Rilke, *Sämtliche Werke* (Insel-Verlag, 1955–66) Band VI, p. 1006; cf. Eudo Mason, *Stichproben: Versuch einer Morphologie der Rilke-Deutung*, in *Orbis Litterarum*, Tome VIII (Copenhagen: 1950) p. 104.
5 Anthony Stephens, *Rainer Maria Rilke's 'Gedichte an die Nacht'* (Cambridge University Press, 1972) pp. 213, 218, 237
6 Else Buddeberg, *Die Duineser Elegien R. M. Rilkes* (Karlsruhe: 1948) p. xxxix.
7 *Lettres françaises à Merline 1919–22* (Paris: 1950) p. 167
8 Edmond Jaloux, *Reconnaissance à Rilke* in *Les Cahiers du Mois* XXIII–XXIV (Paris: 1926).
9 *Rilke et la France* (Paris. Librairie Plon, 1942) pp. 195, 197.
10 Egon Schwarz, *Das verschluckte Schluchzen: Poesie und Politik bei Rainer Maria Rilke* (Athenäum Verlag, 1972).
11 Op. cit., pp. 116, 121.
12 Otto Friedrich Bollnow, *Rilke* (Stuttgart: 1951) pp. 101 ff.
13 Rilke, *Briefe*, Zweiter Band (Briefe aus den Jahren 1914 bis 1926) (Insel-Verlag, 1950) pp. 478 ff.
14 Ida Cermak, *Ich klage nicht, Begegnungen mit der Krankheit in Selbstzeugnissen schöpferischer Menschen* (Wien: 1972). *Rainer Maria Rilke und Marie von Thurn und Taxis: Briefwechsel* (Insel-Verlag, 1951) pp. 954 ff.
15 Sydney Keyes, *Collected Poems* (New York: 1967) p. xxi; Norman Jeffares, *W. B. Yeats* (London: Routledge 1949) p. 338.
16 Rilke, *Sämtliche Werke* [hereinafter S.W.] II, p. 406.
17 S.W. II, p. 511.
18 Walter Falk, *Leid und Verwandlung* (Salzburg: 1961) pp. 92 ff.
19 J. R. von Salis, *Rainer Maria Rilkes Schweizerjahre* (Frauenfeld: 1952) p. 228.

20 *Rainer Maria Rilke – Lou Andreas-Salomé: Briefwechsel* (Zürich: 1952) p. 505.

21 Briefe II, p. 535.

22 Cf. Dieter Bassermann, *Am Rande des Unsagbaren* (Berlin: 1948) p. 13; Elisabeth von Schmidt-Pauli, *R. M. Rilke: Ein Gedenkbuch* (Stuttgart: 1946) p. 20.

23 S.W. II, pp. 82 ff. *Briefe*, Erster Band (Briefe 1897 bis 1914) (Insel-Verlag, 1950) p. 217.

24 *Briefe aus den Jahren 1906–07* (Insel-Verlag, 1930) pp. 206 f., 214; Briefe aus Muzot 1921 bis 1926 (Insel-Verlag, 1940) p. 123.

25 S.W. II, p. 527.

26 S.W. I, p. 637.

27 S.W. I, p. 557.

28 Marie von Thurn und Taxis, *Erinnerungen an R. M. Rilke* (München: 1932) pp. 40 ff.

29 *Briefe* II, pp. 309 f.

30 Ibid., p. 311.

31 Ibid., p. 485.

32 Sidney Keyes, *The Collected Poems* (London: Routledge, 1945) p. 75.

33 W. H. Auden, *In Time of War* (New York: 1939) p. 281.

34 Jacob Steiner, *Rilkes Duineser Elegien* (Bern: 1962).

35 Heinrich Kreutz, *Rilkes Duineser Elegien* (München: 1950).

36 Romano Guardini, *Rainer Maria Rilkes Deutung des Daseins* 1953. English translation by K. G. Knight, *Rilke's Duino Elegies* (London: 1961).

37 *Rilke's Duino Elegies*, p. 179.

38 Ibid., 116.

39 H. F. Peters, *Rainer Maria Rilke: Masks and the Man* (Seattle: 1960) pp. 149 ff.

40 *Rainer Maria Rilke's Duineser Elegien*, ed. E. L. Stahl (Oxford: Blackwell, 1965) pp. ix ff.

41 S.W. II, p. 449.

42 S.W. II, pp. 435 ff.

43 *Briefe* II, p. 35.

44 Especially: Eudo C. Mason, *Lebenshaltung und Symbolik bei Rainer Maria Rilke* (Oxford: 1964; first published 1939); *Rainer Maria Rilke: Sein Leben und sein Werk* (Göttingen: 1964).

45 Especially: Dieter Bassermann, *Der späte Rilke* (München: 1948); *Der andere Rilke* (Bad Homburg: 1961).

46 *Der andere Rilke*, p. 27.

47 *Tagebücher aus der Frühzeit* (Leipzig: 1942) p. 140.

48 Kreutz, op. cit., p. 114; Bassermann, *Der späte Rilke*, p. 107; cf. Stahl, op. cit., p. 36.
49 S.W. II, pp. 130 ff.
50 J. B. Leishman and Stephen Spender, *Duino Elegies*. The German text, with an English translation, introduction and commentary (3rd ed., London: 1948) pp. 133 ff.
51 Op. cit., p. 25.
52 S.W. I, p. 260; *Briefe* I, p. 58.
53 S.W. I, p. 486.
54 S.W. I, pp. 377 f.
55 S.W. II, p. 400.
56 S.W. I, pp. 654 f.
57 *Briefe* I, pp. 76 ff.
58 S.W. I, p. 582.
59 *Briefe* I, pp. 244 f.
60 *Briefe* I, pp. 346, 375.
61 S.W. VI, pp. 924, 937.
62 *Briefe* I, pp. 269 ff.
63 Op. cit., p. 30.
64 *Briefe* II, pp. 200 ff.
65 Edmond Jaloux, *La Dernière Amitié de R. M. Rilke* (Paris: 1949) pp. 58 f.
66 S.W. II, pp. 290 f.
67 *Briefe* I, p. 477; *Briefe* II, p. 351.
68 *Briefe* II, p. 316.
69 *Briefe* I, p. 53.
70 *Briefe* I, pp. 326 f.
71 *Briefe* I, pp. 342 f.
72 *Briefe* I, p. 216; II, p. 265; *Nachlass. Vierte Folge. Die Briefe an Gräfin Sizzo* (Leipzig: 1950) p. 79.
73 *Lettres françaises à Merline*, p. 61.
74 *Briefe* I, pp. 53 ff.
75 Cf. Ursula Emde, *Rilke und Rodin* (Marburg, 1949) pp. 13 ff., 104.
76 Magda von Hattingberg, *Rilke und Benvenuta* (Wien: 1947) p. 87; cf. Mason, *Stichproben*, p. 125.
77 *Briefe* I, p. 23.
78 *Briefe* I, pp. 391 f.
79 *Briefe* I, pp. 71, 95, 250; *Thurn und Taxis Briefwechsel*, p. 42.
80 *Benvenuta*, pp. 23, 40.
81 *Lettres françaises à Merline*, pp. 27 ff., 37 ff., 82, 167, 185.
82 Ibid., pp. 92 ff.
83 S.W. II, pp. 280 f., 299, 306 f.

84 Ibid, p. 291.
85 Ibid., pp. 94 f., 261.
86 Martin Heidegger, *Holzwege* (Frankfurt: 1950) pp. 258 f., 267.
87 S.W. VI, p. 924.
88 S.W. I, p. 260; S.W. VI, p. 936.
89 S.W. II, pp. 130 f.
90 Ibid., p. 466.
91 Ibid., p. 266.
92 Ibid., pp. 174 f.
93 Ibid., pp. 318 f.
94 Ibid., p. 267.
95 Ibid., p. 111.
96 Ibid., p. 466.
97 S.W. I, pp. 659 ff.
98 *Tagebücher aus der Frühzeit*, pp. 36 f.
99 *Briefe* I, p. 172.
100 von Salis, op. cit., p. 108; Maurice Betz, *Rilke in Paris* (Zürich: 1948) pp. 78 f.
101 S.W. VI, p. 942.
102 *Briefe* I, p. 255.
103 *Briefe* I, pp. 363, 370.
104 S.W. VI, p. 728.
105 S.W. VI, p. 756; *Briefe* I, p. 482.
106 *Briefe* I, p. 263.
107 *Briefe* I, p. 380; II, pp. 46, 81.
108 *Briefe* I, p. 368.
109 *Briefe* I, p. 208.
110 *Briefe* I, p. 498.
111 *Briefe* II, pp. 284 ff.
112 *Briefe* II, pp. 68 f.
113 *Briefe* I, p. 376; II, pp. 138 ff.
114 *Briefe* II, pp. 466 ff.
115 Op. cit., pp. 55 ff.
116 *Lettres Milanaises*, ed. Renée Lang (Paris: 1956) p. 78.
117 Op. cit., pp. 27, 84 f., 97.
118 *Tagebücher aus der Frühzeit*, p. 60; Schwarz, op. cit., pp. 69 ff., 78 f.
119 Schwarz, op. cit., pp. 53, 78 f., 107.
120 Op. cit., pp. 22, 98, 103.
121 Peter Demetz, *In Sachen Rainer Maria Rilke und Thomas Mann, Berliner Kritiker-Colloquium* 1965, pp. 4 ff.
122 Op. cit., pp. 52 f., 88 ff., 95 f.
123 Peters, op. cit., p. 177; *Sonnets to Orpheus*. The German text,

with an English translation, introduction and notes by J. B. Leishman (London: 1936) pp. 32 f. Ronald Gray, *The German Tradition in Literature, 1871–1945* (Cambridge University Press, 1965) pp. 248 ff.

124 *Briefe* II, p. 360.
125 *Thurn und Taxis Briefwechsel*, pp. 461 f.
126 *Briefe* II, pp. 16 f.
127 *Lettres françaises à Merline*, pp. 18 ff.
128 *Briefe* II, p. 501.
129 *Lettres françaises à Merline*, p. 122.
130 *Briefe* I, p. 45; II, pp. 275 f.; *Lettres françaises à Merline*, p. 81; Leopold von Schläger, *Rilke auf Capri* (Dresden: 1931) p. 41.
131 *Briefe* I, pp. 214 f.; *Benvenuta*, p. 63.
132 S.W. II, pp. 247, 316.
133 *Briefe* I, pp. 103, 389; II, p. 66.
134 *Briefe* II, pp. 266, 422; Schmidt-Pauli, op. cit., p. 119; S.W. VI, pp. 1036 ff.
135 *Briefe* I, pp. 489 ff; II, pp. 122 f.
136 S.W. II, p. 48; *Briefe* II, p. 455.
137 Mason, *Stichproben*, p. 115; *Briefe* I, pp. 460 f.; S.W. V, p. 33.
138 *Briefe* II, pp. 480 ff.
139 Novalis, *Werke in einem Band*, ed. Wilhelm von Scholz (Stuttgart: 1924) pp. 20 f., 229, 294.
140 *Das Nachleben der Romantik in der modernen deutschen Literatur*, ed Wolfgang Paulsen (Heidelberg: 1969) pp. 130 ff.
141 Stahl, op. cit., p. xxxi.
142 S.W. II, p. 470.
143 *Briefe* II, pp. 107, 332, 365, 496 f.
144 S.W. II, pp. 182 ff.
145 Ibid., pp. 169 f.
146 *Briefe* II, pp. 374, 378 ff.
147 S.W. II, pp. 259 f.
148 Ibid., p. 258.
149 Ibid., pp. 157, 253.
150 Betz, op. cit., pp. 176 ff.; Walther Rehm, *Orpheus: Der Dichter und die Toten* (Düsseldorf: 1950) p. 640.
151 *Briefe* II, pp. 135 ff.; S.W. II, p. 43; *Benvenuta*, p. 157.
152 *Briefe* II, pp. 529 f.; *Tagebücher aus der Frühzeit*, p. 71.
153 *Briefe* I, pp. 157, 273; Schmidt-Pauli, op. cit., p. 246; *Briefe 1906–1907*, p. 129.
154 S.W. II, pp. 60, 241.
155 S.W. II, pp. 530, 557, 563, 568.

156   S.W. II, p. 180; *Briefe* I, pp. 358, 416. Cf. Betz, op. cit., pp. 135 ff.
157   *Briefe aus Muzot*, p. 133.
158   S.W. VI, p. 829; S.W. II, p. 63; *Briefe* II, pp. 491 f.
159   *Briefe* II, p. 358; Betz, op. cit., pp. 167 ff.
160   *Briefe* I, pp. 231, 389, 475.
161   *Nachlass. Vierte Folge*, p. 79.
162   *Briefe* I, p. 477; II, pp. 16, 169, 199.
163   *Briefe* II, pp. 349 ff.
164   *Briefe* II, pp. 406 f.
165   *Briefe* II, p. 363.
166   *Briefe* II, pp. 138 ff.
167   *Briefe* II, p. 68.
168   *Briefe* I, pp. 144, 304; II, p. 38.
169   *Briefe* I, p. 413.
170   S.W. II, pp. 49 ff.; *Thurn und Taxis Briefwechsel*, p. 240.
171   *Briefe* II, pp. 47, 54, 215; *Thurn und Taxis Briefwechsel*, p. xvii; Katharina Kippenberg, *Reiner Maria Rilke: Ein Beitrag* (Leipzig: 1942) p. 164; von Salis, op. cit., p. 83.
172   *Briefe* I, p. 277; II, pp. 284 ff., 395 f.; cf. Rehm, op- cit., p. 420.
173   Mason, *Stichproben*, p. 157.
174   *Briefe* II, pp. 11, 304, 433.
175   *Briefe* II, pp. 294, 326, 378 ff.; S.W. II, p. 519.
176   *Briefe* II, p. 431.
177   S.W. I, pp. 653 f.; II, p. 206.
178   *Briefe* I, p. 277; S.W. I, p. 527; S.W. II, p. 267; von Salis, op. cit., pp. 51 f.
179   S.W. I, p. 531; II, p. 455.
180   S.W. II, pp. 126, 241.
181   *Briefe* I, p. 175; II, pp. 449 f.; *Benvenuta*, p. 78; *Thurn und Taxis Briefwechsel*, p. 324.
182   *Briefe* II, pp. 168 f.; S.W. I, p. 761; *Benvenuta*, p. 68.
183   *Briefe* I, pp. 139, 489; II, pp. 187, 370, 488.
184   *Briefe* I, pp. 209, 272; II, p. 56; S.W. II, p. 449.
185   *Briefe* II, p. 40; cf. Beda Allemann, *Zeit und Figur beim späten Rilke* (Pfullingen: 1961) pp. 25 ff.
186   S.W. II, pp. 43, 257 f.; *Briefe* I, pp. 507 f.
187   *Briefe* I, pp. 97 ff., 402, 411; II, pp. 229 f.; von Salis, op. cit., p. 51.
188   S.W. IV, p. 1028.
189   S.W. II, p. 611.
190   S.W. II, pp. 575, 578, 582, 583, 720.
191   S.W. I, pp. 552 ff.; II, pp. 575, 576, 581.

192 *Briefe* II, p. 245.
193 Briefe II, pp. 297, 340, 352; *Briefe an seinen Verleger* (Insel-Verlag, 1949) p. 49.
194 *Briefe* II, pp. 231 f., 266 f.
195 *Briefe* II, p. 370.
196 *The Truth of Poetry*, p. 110.
197 *Thurn und Taxis Briefwechsel*, pp. 444, 540; *Briefe* II, pp. 60 f.
198 *Briefe* I, pp. 450, 461; II, p. 81.
199 *Briefe* I, p. 256; *Briefe 1902–1906*, p. 274.
200 *Briefe* I, p. v; II, p. 370.
201 *Briefe* II, p. 536.
202 J. B. Leishman, *Sonnets to Orpheus*, p. 179; Mason, *Lebenshaltung*, pp. 21 ff.

Index of Titles or First Lines

Index of Names